SAY YES TO LIFE

Daily Meditations

by
Leo Booth

SCP LIMITED
2700 St. Louis Avenue
Long Beach, CA 90806

ISBN 0-9623282-3-5

This book is dedicated to
all those who are recovering in life.

INTRODUCTION

When I was asked to write this book I was concerned that it should be inclusive, not representing any one religion or denomination and open to every human being who was concerned with discovering their "given" spirituality on a daily basis. I also wanted to represent the compulsive and obsessive behavioral lifestyles that cause pain and distress in a person's life, e.g., eating disorders, gambling, adult children issues, and people who love others too much! At times it felt as if I was wearing more than one hat but I was surprised at the comfort of the fit.

These meditations are personal and I do not apologize for the use of the personal pronoun "I". They recount my struggle with a variety of topics and because human beings are so similar, I have little doubt that you will be able (regardless of background) to identify with the feelings and struggles expressed.

Talking about God is always difficult, and reference to the "gender" of God has become a serious issue among many concerned Christians, particularly the feminist groups that have (quite correctly) felt ignored, abused and discounted. Sufficient to say that I believe God to be sexless, religionless and beyond any culture, class or creed.

In earlier editions, I used the masculine pronoun to refer to God, just to be consistent. In this years since this book was originally published, I have become more aware of the effects of language on the image people carry of God. In this edition, I refer to God as God, or Creator, in order to truly make this book inclusive. I've also made other slight alterations to similarly make the text more "gender-friendly." No other changes have been made.

Talking about God from the human standpoint always reflects our smallness and imperfection, and yet the fact that we can talk about God at all reveals our inherent greatness.

This book is not intended to convert people from their personal beliefs or convictions, but to show on a daily basis the connection between our daily lives as recovering people (whatever the addiction) with the God-given dynamic of spirituality. How we struggle with what it is to be a human being. How we fight, cry, surrender and succeed all in a single day. And how God is involved.

For the recovering "compulsive person" God is too important to miss — may you find God now. This book is dedicated to all who are recovering from life.

SAY YES TO LIFE

Daily Meditations

Leo Booth

SCP Limited
Long Beach, CA 90806

The one serious
conviction that a
man should have is
that nothing is to be
taken seriously.

Nicholas Murray Butler

*"It is not that I think or believe [in spirituality]
but that I know."*

Sir Arthur Conan Doyle

Some things I seem to know intuitively: and I know that spirituality is involved in and affects everything. In a human being it combines the physical, mental and emotional states, but it also reaches beyond the human being and connects the peoples of the world. Spirituality is the force for good and wholeness in this universe.

This is not just an opinion or a thought. It is a feeling that runs so deep in my being that I know it must be true. When I read, hear music or see movies, this feeling is often evoked, and I know God is alive in God's world and wanting it to be ONE.

In the silence of Your world I know You.

"A thing is not necessarily true because a man dies for it."

Oscar Wilde

I came to the conclusion in my battle with alcoholism that my involvement with God's will for me was crucial; my choice is the result of God's bestowed gift of freedom. And freedom is awfully real! The price of freedom is Auschwitz; the price of freedom is the world's starving millions; the price of freedom is the dead drunk in a derelict building. People do insane and destructive things, usually because they think they know best. They die to protect their egos. The sin of Adam, wanting to be like God, haunts us all.

Today I am learning to detach spiritually in order to discover a pure and selfless love. I stand back and consider before I act; often after a time of reflection I see the event differently ... and it is okay to change my mind.

Lord, I understand choice to be the key to my humanity.

"No man is an island, entire of itself; every man is a piece of the continent, a part of the main."

John Donne

For years I thought that I was alone; lost isolated and afraid. Today I understand this to be a symptom of my alcoholism, an aspect of my disease. Alcoholism is "cunning, baffling and powerful"; it is a mystery that we have only begun to understand. One thing we know, the disease, the "ism" of alcoholism, involves more than the act of drinking. Feelings of inadequacy, isolation and fear keep us from recovering until we discover the spiritual strength to confront the disease in our lives. The initial risk of letting go and trusting others is an essential part of the recovery process.

When we discover that we are not alone, then relationships and hope are reactivated; life is worth living again.

O Lord, I believe I am part of this world and an important part of You.

"A hungry man is not a free man."

Adlai Stevenson

For years I craved food. It was my escape from reality. It stopped the pain, loneliness and anger — for a moment. It felt good. Eventually I began to feel bad — but I could not stop. I was addicted to sugar. My freedom was being exchanged for doughnuts!

I heard a man talk about his compulsion around cocaine and gambling. I asked how he managed to abstain and he replied: "Talk about it, a day at a time!"

Today I am compulsive about getting well, and I talk about my disease every day. The price of freedom is vulnerability. God is in the risk. I have taken it.

God, let me experience freedom in the choices I make today.

*"It's the most unhappy people who most
fear change."*

Mignon McLaughlin

W hen I was drinking, I hated change. I hated things not being the same. I feared anything being different. Rarely did I want to go anywhere new. My attitudes were fixed and rigid. I resented any criticism of my behavior. The unexpected was seen as sabotage or a threat. My paranoia was extreme.

Today I have decided to let go of the control, the pretense and the arrogance. I face life as it comes — and today I do not drink. I am responsible for my life but I cannot control the world. Today I am learning to relax in the acceptance of my disease.

*May I always discover the courage to change the
things I can.*

"Nothing is interesting if you are not interested."

Helen MacInnes

There is a subtle distinction between "dry" alcoholics and "sober" alcoholics. Sober alcoholics choose not to drink because they have accepted their alcoholism. Dry alcoholics are not drinking but are invariably angry and resentful — and they are not expressing these feelings. Their abstinence is not exciting because they are not interested in it — they are bored.

Dry alcoholics are also boring to be around. Why? Because they are bored. Their boredom makes them boring. They really want to drink. They have stopped drinking for reasons that do not include the acceptance of the disease. Thus, they are still victims of the disease.

Sobriety, by contrast, is an adventure into self. It greets the new day with enthusiasm and energy. Sobriety is the spiritual discovery of God in our lives.

Let me always remember that my interests in life reflect my interest in You.

"I could not say I believe. I know! I have had the experience of being gripped by something that is stronger than myself, something that people call God."

Carl Jung

God is beyond our comprehension, and in a sense we are all agnostics — none of us KNOW know; uncertainty is part of faith.

However, there are moments when God is alive and vivid in new and stimulating experiences that are beyond explanation other than — "that's God". Loving relationships, friendships, the beauty of nature, the complexities of life and the universe; not to mention music, poetry and the human conscience: all speak of God. History is full of holy people who carry the message: God is love and is to be discovered in our love of self and others.

God, known and yet incomprehensible, help me to discover You in my doubts and confusions.

*"I haven't understood a bar of music in my life,
but I have felt it."*

Igor Stravinsky

It is okay not to understand.

A miracle is not to be understood but experienced.
So much in life we will never understand and there
is growth in confusion. We are not perfect. We will
never be perfect. The mystery of life is exactly that
— a mystery.

As an alcoholic I often sought to appear "as God". I
had to have an answer for everything, even if I made
up the answer! Not to know was humiliating for me
because it took away control, my need to be in
charge, my hopeless and exhausting quest for
perfection. With the failure to be perfect came the
guilt, shame and anger.

Today I am able to live with life's daily confusions
— and it's okay!

*Lord, help me never to lose touch with the feelings
that keep me human.*

*"Extremists think that 'communication' means
agreeing with them."*

Leo Rosten

As an alcoholic I was an extremist. I was not
only compulsive and obsessive about alcohol, but I
became compulsive and obsessive about my
opinions, my thoughts and my attitude towards life.
Anybody who disagreed with me was wrong or a
fool! I only listened to those who were saying what I
wanted to hear.

For years I played at being God. But that spiritual
part of me, that I believe exists in all of us, was
isolated and unhappy with this behavior. Although
I would never admit it, I knew that often I was
wrong, bull--headed and in pain. I would spend
sleepless nights thinking how I could say I was sorry
without apologizing! For years my pride and ego
kept me sick and unhappy.

Today I appreciate those who have a different view
on life. Today I can disagree with my neighbor
without carrying a grudge. Today I can live with
difference.

*I pray that I may always hear what my opponent
is saying.*

"If Negro freedom is taken away, or that of any minority group, the freedom of all the people is taken away."

Paul Robeson

As a recovering alcoholic I belong to a minority. As somebody with the disease of addiction I am aware of my difference. And I have experienced prejudice and injustice because I was not born like other people.

But in a spiritual sense the acceptance of my disease has given me a freedom that united me with other minorities, other "different" groups, the countless shades of humanity. My disease has produced a spiritual unity and bond with creation that makes me rejoice in my difference and produces a tolerance of others that was not there before. In this sense I thank God for my dis--ease.

You, who made the different, also created the unity; help me find both in my life.

> *"To teach men how to live without certainty and yet without being paralyzed by hesitation is perhaps the chief thing philosophy can do."*
>
> *Bertrand Russell*

I suppose the Twelve Steps are a practical philosophy of how to live positively with the disease of alcoholism: (a) Don't drink. (b) Find a God in your life that is understandable. (c) Begin to make positive choices in attitudes and behaviors. (d) Let "Never forget" be an essential part of the message.

The miracle of this philosophy is that it reaches out to so many who suffer with addictive compulsions and teaches us how to live with being imperfect. I believe the Twelve Steps are the answer to "The Fall" of humanity — we are going home to God.

Let me see beyond the logic to Your loving energy.

*"The aim of education is the knowledge not of fact,
but of values."*

Dean William R. Inge

Facts can sometimes confuse. They can be used
to hide behind. They can be manipulated into lies.
Facts are no substitute for values — human values.

Today I not only value my life but I value life itself.
When I walk amongst nature, I taste its purity,
observe its beauty, experience its strength — and I
know I am a part of it all. Today my values have
changed because I see myself as "part of" rather
than "separate from". I belong to this universe, this
world, this planet and what I do affects the essential
value of life. With my daily respect for self comes a
respect for property, people, different cultures and
God.

Today the things I truly value I do not pay for; the
things I cherish cannot be won or bought.
Spirituality is free.

*Teach me to value the meaning of freedom and the
richness of life.*

"Treat the other man's faith gently; it is all he has to believe with."

Henry Hoskins

I said that I was a nonviolent drunk. Today I am able to see that I was sarcastic and verbally violent, and this was no less painful or destructive to the victim. A target for my anger and venom was the faith and beliefs of others, especially when they differed radically from my own. My alcoholism made me a prejudiced and bigoted man, a prisoner of my arrogance.

My sobriety teaches me to be accepting and tolerant of the views and opinions of others. A spirituality that embraces everyone, rather than a narrow and restrictive religion, is my prescription for life. I have exchanged bigotry for freedom, and I am happy in God's world.

I pray that my acceptance of others, regardless of culture or creed, may lead to understanding.

"The fault is in us."

Hannah Arendt

As a drunk I would blame everybody for my problems: My family was too controlling. I did not have people around who understood me. I worked too hard and the people were too demanding. The weather was awful!

Today I accept my involvement with my past predicament. Bad things happened to me because I created them in my life. And this means that good and creative things can also happen in my life if I create them. I need not remain the problem. I can be the solution!

*Let me discover Your answer in my response
to life.*

> *"Few people are capable of expressing with equanimity, opinions which differ from the prejudices of their social environment."*
>
> *Albert Einstein*

P art of my growth in sobriety is learning to say no. For years I tried to please everybody with the result that I pleased very few and became exhausted in the process! I have learned that sometimes I need to be unpopular in order to remain serene; unpopular to practice my spiritual program.

To understand the gift of God's creation requires the acceptance that we are not the same and, as people, we will have different opinions and attitudes. Truth has many shades. To be unpopular at times is reality; truth is always real.

I pray that I might always say and do what I believe to be right, regardless of public opinion.

"You cannot build a reputation on things you are going to do."

Mabel Newcomber

Procrastination is the addicts' game. I will give up alcohol tomorrow. Soon I will take an inventory of my eating habits. Later I will express my anger and pain. Tomorrow and tomorrow — but it never happens!

The tragedy is that we not only bring pain and problems into our lives but we keep them there. Recovery requires action; sobriety and the spiritual program demand movement.

Today I will talk about my pain.

"Creative intelligence in its various forms and activities is what makes man."

James Harvey Robinson

Spirituality is being a positive and creative human being in all areas of my life; this I know to be true today. I am not only creative, I am a creative human being. God created me to create. I am a part of God's love for the world; through me great and wonderful events can happen. Although I am not divine, I know that I share divinity. I am special.

But with this knowledge comes tremendous responsibility because things are only going to happen if I make them happen in my life. To know that I am creative does not make me creative. I have to do something, make something, create something in my life.

Today I work at my life like a carpenter works with wood. I chip away those things I do not want; I smooth down the rough areas of my life, and I polish up those things I want people to see. I accept responsibility for my creativity, and I thank God, on a daily basis, for it.

Teach me, O Creator of the universe, to use my life as a tool for goodness, joy and truth.

17

"Gluttony is not a secret vice."

Orson Welles

T he unspoken disease of food: hide in food, bury anger with food, cry behind food. Food addiction — eating, forever dieting, starving — is the hidden disease that is becoming more obvious. But are we talking about it? Recovering alcoholics minimize it and get lost in ice cream and doughnuts. For many people the pain around food is as real as alcohol or any other drug. The family and relationships suffer.

Today I am willing to talk about it. Spirituality affects all my life and this involves my eating habits and body weight. God does not make junk and so I choose not to eat junk. Today I choose to talk about the buried emotions that I am stuffing behind the food. That is a step towards living.

When I bless the food at meal time, may I also bless my abstinence.

*"Treat all men alike. Give them all the same
laws. Give them all an even chance to live
and grow."*

Chief Joseph

Today it is important for me to remember that I
am not the only human being in this universe; I
need to respect and be considerate of others.
Spirituality requires that I treat all people with
dignity and respect because they carry something of
God within them — the image of God is with all
people. In this way I show and give respect to self.

As an alcoholic I was selfish and demanding,
wanting my way all the time. Sobriety teaches me
that "the way" must include others; my fellow
humans are part of my life and journey. I cannot live
in isolation and be sober.

*O Spirit of the World, teach me to respect others,
because in this way, I respect myself.*

"One person with a belief is equal to a force of ninety--nine who have only interest."

John Stuart Mill

I believe in sobriety because it works for me. I believe in sobriety because it makes me feel good about myself. I believe in sobriety because it has enabled me to rejoin the human race; I was so tired of feeling lonely, ashamed and isolated.

Also this belief I have in me has rekindled a positive relationship with my higher power. Today God is a friend. Today I understand more about what God wants for me. Today I am broad enough in my thinking to find God in anything that is positive and creative — from music to hugs in the park!

Belief has developed with my spiritual program, and I am able to face the daily pains and conflicts of life. Today I know what it is to be a winner — and, thank God, it doesn't mean I have to be perfect or in control.

Thank You for the gift of my believing in myself.

"The price of freedom of religion or of speech or of the press is that we must put up with, and even pay for, a good deal of rubbish."

Justice Robert Jackson

I need to be tolerant in my sobriety. I need to allow others to say what they feel and live according to their standards.

I was intolerant towards people who were different from myself. Much of what I criticized yesterday, I accept today; some things I still reject.

To love someone should not require sameness; equally, I can accept people without agreeing with what they say or how they behave. Disagreements and conflicts lead to growth; change requires a variety of forces.

Not everything I say or do is pure — and that has become the key to the acceptance of others. My history teaches me that I benefit from the variety of opinions that are represented in humankind.

God, You have created many ways to Truth, may I appreciate them through the experiences of others.

"Poetry is not an assertion of truth, but the making of that truth more fully real to us."

T. S. Eliot

God is able to communicate in a thousand different ways and one such way is poetry.

Spirituality is discovering God in creation, and this involves more than religion or denominationalism. Spirituality is a comprehensive approach to God's world and is the unifying factor at the center of the universe. Spirituality is about what is true — wherever it is found in the world.

Poetry and other art forms become part of the spiritual journey for us as we struggle to understand and communicate Truth.

In poetry may I find an expression of Your love for me; in my use of poetry, may I express my love for You.

"Sleep that knots up the ravelled sleave of care."
William Shakespeare

When I was new in my recovery from alcoholism I was told to remember the letters H.A.L.T.: Do not get too Hungry, Angry, Lonely or Tired.

Sleep is something my body needs, and even if I do not always know it, my body does. The tiredness in my body is telling me to slow down. Sleep is part of my spiritual program because it enables me to feel rested, invigorated and alive. Through sleep I am able to be creative and positive in my life — showing a practical love to my body. Sleep is one way I take care of myself!

Thank You for the joy and rest that comes with sleep.

"Too many people are thinking of security instead of opportunity; they seem more afraid of life than death."

James Byrnes

Today I am aware of the opportunities that I did not recognize when I was drinking. Drinking stopped me from seeing the life that was before me. I drank myself away from the daily miracle. I missed the sunsets, the fun of relationships, the joy of the theater and the satisfaction of being aware.

In the business world I did not see the opportunity for profit and expansion; I did not create or have faith in my ideas, and I was not able to understand or absorb the new information to be successful in my life. Alcoholism kept me on the outside of my life.

Today I am alive in my life, creating, expanding and enjoying my leisure. With sobriety I have the opportunity to experience God in the many aspects of life.

Teach me to find You in the risks of life.

"Honesty is the first chapter of the book of wisdom."

Thomas Jefferson

It is impossible to have a spiritual program without being honest. It is impossible to be recovering from addiction without being honest. An aspect of sobriety is honesty.

Today I can see that I was never really known when I was using because I was so dishonest. I stopped other people from getting to know me. I stopped me from getting to know me. Part of my pain involved my dishonesty; part of my loneliness and feelings of isolation was caused by my dishonesty; the unmanageability that nearly destroyed my life grew in my dishonesty.

Today I need to be honest, rigorously honest, even in the small things. I can no longer exist to please others. I need to please myself. I need to love myself by being honest.

O God of wisdom, let me find truth in the honesty of my own life.

"The ablest men in all walks of modern life are men of faith."

Bruce Barton

It is important for those of us who have been crushed by the disease of addiction to have faith that life will get better. We stopped using or being co--dependent because the behavior was destroying us. Our lives were disintegrating in negative behavior and attitudes. Now we have chosen a different way to live.

Today I seek to find God in my freedom of choice, my ability to change. I have faith in the daily belief that my life will get better so long as I avoid those things that hurt me. My faith enables me to change.

O God, my faith in me reflects my belief in You.

"Sexual pleasure, wisely used and not abused, may prove the stimulus and liberator of our finest and most exalted activities."

Havelock Ellis

Sex is most beautiful because it enables the human being to experience and give love at an intimate and personal level. It also combines all the spiritual senses of body, mind and feeling in one expression, balancing tenderness with strength, patience with desire, need with selflessness.

Also the awareness and experience of a beautiful sexuality should be taken into all other manifestations of life — work, leisure, friendship, sports and prayer.

The gift of sex is one of our finest and most creative attributes and leads to all that is noble in people, therefore, it should not be used irresponsibly. Today I understand that I have a responsibility to the gifts that God has shared with me.

May I find in my sexuality an awareness of You.

"Education today, more than ever before, must see clearly the dual objectives: education for living and education for making a living."

James Mason Wood

T he spiritual life is a productive life. Not only does it make for a prosperous life in every sense of the word, but it makes for a creative lifestyle. Nothing is wasted on spiritual people; they learn from their mistakes and doubts.

For too long I was stunted in my spiritual growth by negative and destructive thinking. I became dependent upon a sick self and attracted equally sick people. I used my education and knowledge to keep people out and remained isolated. I needed to change. I wanted to change. But how? As with everything else in life I needed to imitate those who were successful. I needed to be shown how to live a different way. I needed to discover the power of my spirituality. I found successful people. They helped me. Today I am able to help myself.

I pray for the knowledge to imitate those who are successful in life.

"Success is a journey not a destination."

Ben Sweetland

So long as I am sober I know that I am successful. But I also know that my sobriety is more than keeping away from the first drink. My sobriety requires that I be a creative and successful human being in all areas of my life — in my relationships, at work, with my family, my business ventures and in my acts of charity. The road to success is exactly that — it is a road that I am traveling along, and I will be on it until the day I die. I suppose the danger is in thinking that I have arrived. Then I get complacent and apathetic, I slow down and the energy for recovery is diminished.

Today I know that I am successful so long as I keep moving along with my spiritual program.

Let me always be confident as I walk in my journey of life.

"Treat people as if they were what they ought to be, and you help them to become what they are capable of being."

Johann W. von Goethe

My program of recovery from alcoholism helps me have a relationship with myself and helps me relate to and understand others. The more I understand my strengths and weaknesses, the more I am able to understand others.

Any understanding of spirituality involves other people. If spirituality helps me become what God intends for me, then this is also true for others. Today I choose to treat myself and other people as children of God, remembering that we were created to reach for the skies!

Lord, our potential forever rests in You.

"We have the power to make this the best generation of mankind in the history of the world — or to make it the last."

John F. Kennedy

War is tragic because it always destroys; it kills creation itself. People, buildings, relationships, trust, hope, culture, history, youth — they all disappear behind a puff of smoke. The immensity of war is such that it cannot be fully comprehended. Only isolated aspects can be understood: a child is maimed, a treaty is broken, a race is blamed, bullets are heard and a history that existed within a human life is ended in silence.

Addiction is a kind of war — a silent war that exists within an individual and family. People, trust, buildings, hope, culture, history and youth disappear behind a glass or a pill. Creation is attacked from the inside; God is forgotten in an act of destructive selfishness.

Teach me to make peace in my life.

*"We have just enough religion to make us hate,
but not enough to make us love one another."*

Jonathan Swift

Religion is a powerful influence in the world, but so often the power is negative. It has been used to judge, divide, separate and control people; rob them of their freedom and creativity; chain them to creeds and teachings that are not comprehensible. Unfortunately, religion has become dull and lifeless for many people and God's love is missed.

But the power of creative spirituality is alive in God's world. It unites and frees the people so that they can be discovered in their individuality. Difference is accepted, choice is respected and healing is perceived in our ability to love.

*Let me ever bring the gift of God's spirituality to
those who have misplaced it.*

"We work to become, not to acquire."

Elbert Hubbard

I believe it is easier to get well than it is to stay sick — but we must be prepared to work for our sobriety. We need to confront the disease and discover the person that God created. The road to recovery is rewarding because we cast aside those aspects of our character that have been destroying us and discover our strengths, virtues and God-given spirituality.

For years I worked for money or for security or for acclaim — today I am working on myself for myself. I work at discovering God in God's world, and I am also finding God in my life. I realize that my creative work coincides with God's will for the world.

Thank You for the gift of work that enables me to discover more of me.

"There are three kinds of lies: lies, damned lies and statistics."

Benjamin Disraeli

I used to be able to hide behind anything — even statistics. Figures, and the quoting of figures, can expand the ego and keep you sick. They can confuse the issues by making everything complicated.

In the field of alcoholism statistics are important for comparison and research but they can never be a substitute for a rigorous honesty that is based upon personal experience. I do not think that statistics alone stopped a person from drinking, but the sharing of a personal suffering and victory can produce an identification that leads to change.

As a recovering alcoholic I need to know the statistics concerning my disease but I also need to know that today's recovery is based upon yesterday's honest sharing.

Let me always see the faces behind the numbers.

> *"The brighter you are, the more you have to learn."*
>
> *Don Herold*

The one thing I know in sobriety is how much I do not know! I thought I knew every thing about God because I was a priest, only to discover that I had made God a prisoner of the Church. Once I was willing to free God from my prison, I discovered a freedom and awareness that daily fascinates and astounds me.

Today I see that the glory of God shines within my pain, within my loneliness, within my confusion, and the acceptance of my disease is the key to recovery. Today the suffering enables me to discover a realistic spirituality — and it is okay to be confused!

With each new day, Lord, let me learn something ... even if it is that I have not learned anything that day!

*"Capital, as such, is not evil; it is its wrong use
that is evil."*

Mohandas K. Gandhi

Today I am not afraid to say that I am concerned
for my prosperity — not just in terms of health,
friendship and employment but also concerning
money. For years I was concerned to have the best,
buy the best, own the best and not shortchange
myself — yet I felt guilty in having such feelings.
Today in my sobriety I truly believe that I deserve
the best. In this way I am loving myself. Money,
prosperity and capital are not bad in themselves; it is
how we use them.

Today, as promised in my recovery, things are
certainly getting better and I am able to invest and
buy wisely. Some years ago I would squander
money on my addiction. Today I am able to
appreciate and share my monetary benefits. Family,
friends and the needy can genuinely share my
prosperity: the more I give away today, the more I
get.

*Thank You for all the many benefits You have
showered upon me in my recovery, not least capital.
May I always use it responsibly.*

"Christ cannot possibly have been a Jew. I don't have to prove that scientifically. It is a fact!"

Joseph Goebbels

Today I know that if a lie is said loudly enough, often enough, with ceremony and ritual, people will believe it. I can identify with the above statement: I said I was not alcoholic because I did not drink every day, in the mornings, all day and I was too young! People believed me. Some people still choose to believe this lie.

Spirituality requires that I not only confront the lies in other people but also in myself. Usually if I am angry at the remarks of others, it is because they remind me of myself. Today I seek not simply to condemn but to understand.

May I continue to learn from the criticism I make of others.

"In every child who is born, under no matter what circumstances, and of no matter what parents, the potentiality of the human race is born again."

James Agee

Today I am able to believe and see the God-given dignity of the human race in the faces and lifestyles of others. In the challenge and rebelliousness of youth is the hope for tomorrow.

Today I can associate myself with the need to question, risk and be outrageous. Today I can play, laugh at myself and own my craziness. Today I do not need to be perfect.

When I used drugs, I was so judgmental, serious and controlling. Everything had to have a place, or an answer, or be acceptable to others. My moments of guilt were caused by my inability to please others.

Today I can be childlike and identify with the radical message for tomorrow:" To thine own self be true!"

I see a child looking at the stars and I smile; I am that child.

*"The hopeful man sees success where others see
failure, sunshine where others see shadows
and storm."*

O. S. Marden

Spirituality involves our attitudes and
perceptions as well as our prayers. Spirituality
requires a realistic awareness of what we need and
what we have been given. Spirituality sees beyond
the problems into the solution.

Hope is a feeling that is based on a spiritual
perception of life that shuns apathy and negativity.
Everything can be used for good if it is perceived
realistically; destructive experiences, painful
moments and failed relationships can all be used to
create a new tomorrow.

The hope that stems from our ability to change
requires a realistic understanding of what has
happened. No aspect of life should be wasted
because it can point to a glorious tomorrow.

*Teach me to discover the secret of success in the
problems of life.*

*"Love your neighbor as thyself, but choose
your neighbor."*

Louise Beal

P art of my recovery and sobriety involves
change. It is not enough to put down the jug to gain
sobriety; I need to make substantial changes in my
life.

Where I live, with whom I live, the friends I keep
and the relationships I make are crucial to my
sobriety. Human beings imitate. They imitate
clothes, hairstyles and mannerisms. Sobriety is also
imitated.

As a recovering alcoholic, I can only be spiritually
happy with those who are joyous and free; I need to
find them.

*God, You are to be found in Your creation. Let me
seek You in a noble lifestyle.*

*"Nothing is more terrible than activity
without insight."*

Thomas Carlyle

I believe that recovery can only begin when we see
or start to get a glimpse of who we are and what we
are dealing with insight: an insight into self.

However, the moment we begin to see must be
followed by a determined effort to discover more;
digging through the denial, pain and manipulation
to the disease. Then after discovering the disease in
our lives, we must be prepared to risk talking about
it — on a daily basis.

Recovery requires a daily desire to see, discover and
talk about our addiction — with this insight comes
recovery.

*You are the light of the world; shine through my
honesty.*

"When a man has pity on all living creatures, then only is he noble."

Buddha

We all need each other. More than this, we need to help and sustain each other. And this concept extends beyond human beings — the world is full of other creatures that God has made and which make our lives so fascinating and entertaining. Animals and plants make up our ecological history and yet so often we rob and hurt our environment.

Recovery from alcoholism means more than putting down the drink. Today I am picking up a responsible attitude that makes me care, on a spiritual level, for my world.

God, as I look around my world I cannot help but worship You.

"Freedom comes from human beings, rather than from laws and institutions."

Clarence Darrow

The disease of alcoholism does not live in bottles or books. It lives in people. Drug problems are people problems. Sobriety exists in the person, not the theory.

In this sense recovery must be experienced, rather than simply talked about. The Program is essentially not written in books or taught in lecture rooms but is lived in the lives of people; the Program stems from the heart.

I believe the program is that spark of divinity that God has bestowed upon all of us ... and we must discover it within.

Teach me to remember that to think a smile without revealing a smile is to be grumpy.

*"It is the chiefest point of happiness that man is
willing to be what he is."*

Desiderious Erasmus

I am an alcoholic. Today I am able to love myself
because I am able to accept myself.

More than this: because I am able to accept myself,
I am able to be myself. The acceptance of my
disease around alcohol has taught me that I am not
perfect, and I do not live in a perfect world — this
leads to an acceptance of others. My pain around
alcohol has given me an insight into the sufferings
of others ... and this has produced spiritual growth.

I am happy not because I am an alcoholic but
because I know that I am an alcoholic. Today I can
be what I was meant to be, rather than the fake that
I was becoming.

In the spiritual journey is the happiness.

"Let there be spaces in your togetherness."
                                        Kahlil Gibran

As an alcoholic I demanded love and was possessive of others. I had a selfish love that treated people as possessions, for my own satisfaction and survival. I was claustrophobic in my affection and smothered any creative love; my fear of being alone made me blackmail people with my needs and emotions.

Today I can love people while still allowing them to breathe. An important part of my program is detachment; I take responsibility for me and I allow others to take responsibility for themselves. I give the people I love space.

Sometimes I need to love people enough to let them go. Spiritually I am beginning to understand that in order to be free, I must give freedom to others.

God, in the spaces of my love is the growth experienced.

"I am a man; nothing human is alien to me."

Terence

Humility is not so much about trying to be good as accepting that I am imperfect. For too long I thought that humility was keeping the peace, appearing to be perfect, bottling up my anger and resentments — living a life of people-pleasing.

Today I understand that humility is being real. It is accepting my humanity and being honest in my relationships. Humility is respecting the lives of others but also respecting my own. Humility is seeking to reveal that divinity that God has given to my life. Humility is knowing that in the lives of my fellow humans, — the good and the bad — is me.

Master, let me have the humility to be real.

*"The Bible tells us to love our neighbors and also
to love our enemies; probably because they are
generally the same people."*

G. K. Chesterton

The spiritual program that I embrace makes me
look to where I am, rather than where I want to be. I
must live in the now, rather than the never--never--
land of tomorrow.

To love my world I need to seek to understand
those people who live in my world. To love my
world involves an acceptance of those who are
different than me. I must seek to build bridges,
rather than barriers. It is so easy for me to talk about
loving and being concerned for the starving
millions and forgetting to love and relate to the co--
worker in my office or the neighbor down the
street.

I have some experience of people who can be
difficult because I lived with the addicted me for
many years; I am the key to my enemies.

*Teach me to accept in love those who, for today, I do
not like.*

47

*"But one day when I was sitting quiet and feeling
like a motherless child, which I was, it came to me
that feeling of being part of everything, not separate
at all. I knew that if I cut a tree,
my arm would bleed."*

Alice Walker

Today I am aware of the truth that I belong. I am an essential part of God's world. I share divinity because God made me. Today I choose to seek that spiritual center in me that is forever positive and creative. Today I am the center of my universe.

Past hurts and wrongs cannot take away the uniqueness in my life. Past abuses and painful put--downs, my years of alternating between the lost child and the scapegoat in my family need not make me a victim today. Today I am free to choose recovery and an acceptance of self. Today I choose to associate with the winners of this world. Today I participate in creation by being a creative person for me. Yesterday's pain need not have any power in my life today.

*When I kneel before the stream, mountains and
stars, I feel me.*

"The life of the law has not been logic; it has been experience."

Oliver Wendell Holmes, Jr.

Today I respect the law. In this way I respect the society in which I live. I am not "an island unto myself". I live in a community and have a responsibility to myself and that community — such is sobriety.

For years I did what I wanted and tried not to be found out. I was manipulative, dishonest and unhappy; to stay sick is depressing and exhausting

Then I decided to remove the pain. I accepted the disease and began to change my life. I discovered the spiritual law of freedom with responsibility. Law is the collective experience of the many who choose to live a certain way, and today I choose to live amongst them. My understanding of spirituality involves respecting the laws that give me the dignity of citizenship.

O Lord, help me to see that in the laws of civilization is the gift of freedom.

"The chief cause of human errors is to be found in the prejudices picked up in childhood."

Rene Descartes

During the past few years I have begun to recognize how many of my prejudices were planted in childhood. Family, teachers, priests and the neighborhood passed on to me prejudices: "The Jews are bad because they killed Jesus." "Blacks are inferior to white people — but you should be kind to them." "Women should obey the man of the house." "Gays are child molesters." "People who do not accept Jesus will not go to Heaven." "Sex is for having babies and you should not enjoy it."

Today I live with the problem of knowing that these statements are untrue but a part of me is still affected by them.

Today my spiritual program demands that I expose prejudice for the hate--mail that it is, and try to pass on to the next generation the joy that comes from love, acceptance and freedom.

Let the children grow in freedom.

> *"Going to Church doesn't make you a Christian*
> *any more than going to the garage makes*
> *you a car."*
>
> Laurence J. Peter

I cannot help but believe that the truth of Christianity is about bringing the world and humankind together, rather than creating divisions and resentments. It must be much bigger than what we do or say in any building. Christ's truth seeks to discover God in the splendor of this varied world. In this sense, Christianity is an aspect of the world's spirituality!

My addiction made me a small man with a small god. Constantly focusing on the differences in the world stopped me from seeing the glaring similarities; my exclusiveness kept me a lonely man. The world of black and white, rather than shades of creative color, is a sick and dangerous world to live in. Jesus Christ reveals for me the "man for others"; the bridge by which reconciliation and harmony can be achieved. His message for me is not so much a series of dogmas as a revealed journey into Truth.

In the created stranger, help me to discover the
friend.

"Only work which is the product of inner
compulsion can have spiritual meaning."

Walter Gropius

I have developed, in my recovery, an awareness of the beauty of this world and an appreciation of what people can produce. Sobriety has made art accessible. Today I can see beauty in paintings, sculpture, music, literature and the natural art of nature.

Spirituality is always creative and it is at the center of all that is good, noble and inspiring. Although I am not an artist, I can appreciate and have a feeling of belonging to the beauty of this world — in a sense it all happens and takes shape through me. The rediscovery of spirituality has brought the world and the universe into my life.

Help me to have the desire to recreate Your
splendors through my experiences.

*"For us, patriotism is the same as the love
of humanity."*

Mohandas Gandhi

Today I am on the side of humankind. I am convinced that my welfare is generated by the peace and stability of the world. The love and joy that produces spiritual growth stems from my relationships in the world: we cannot exist alone.

Today I strive to bring the world and people together; we must not seek to be the same but rather rejoice in the richness of difference.

Drugs always divide, separate and isolate; spirituality unites. Today I am an optimist for humankind because of what has happened in my own life.

Thank You for a humanity that can be shared.

*"I was a free--thinker before I knew
how to think."*

George Bernard Shaw

All of us are influenced by somebody. Not to be influenced is to remain ignorant. Most of us hinder our thinking, particularly around spiritual things, because of pride. We don't like change. We find it hard to accept attitudes and opinions that differ from our own. Pride keeps us deaf and often stupid. However, the daily program of a lived spirituality encourages a variety of opinions and attitudes. We can learn from different customs, lifestyles and religions. We can be helped in our understanding of life by the stranger.

I know that I do not have all the answers. Perhaps you carry my answers. Today I am prepared to listen to you.

*God, the sustainer of all religions and philosophies,
help us to discover You in our differences.*

"Wherever two people meet, there are really six people present. There is each man as he sees himself, each man as the other person sees him, and each man as he really is."

William James

P art of my spiritual journey involves the discovery of self. For years I pretended to be what I was not; for years I pretended to be what I imagined myself to be; for years I pretended to be what you wanted me to be — always my real self eluded me.

Today I am beginning to know myself. I know my needs. I understand my strengths. I accept my weaknesses and I live with my confusions. From the time I decided to put down the glass of alcohol, it progressively got better — but there is still a great deal I do not understand. Inhumanity, the daily violence and suffering, my own personal greed, cowardice and arrogance — where does it come from? I don't know and today that is okay. However, I still search; my suspicion is that the answer lies within my own insecurities.

In Your time, God, may I grow in my understanding of self.

"The child without ambition is like a watch with a broken spring."

R. W. Stockman

It is not wrong to have ambition. It is not wrong to want to be somebody. The tragedy is that this has to be said!

For too long we have played the tapes in our head that discouraged ambition and creative pride. We confused humility with timidity and self--abuse. We waited for things to happen, rather than made them happen.

Today I know that I am a creature of God — created to create. God is at work in my life. I am part of God's miracle for the world.

O God, may I always have ambition for those things that are good and true.

"Each honest calling, each walk of life, has its own elite, its own aristocracy based upon excellence of performance."

James Bryant Conant

Each of us has a gift and a special feature that is unique to ourselves. Unfortunately so many people are so busy admiring the gifts of others that they miss their own; they are so caught up in the lives of others that they miss the specialness of their own existence. One of the symptoms of my alcoholism was low self-esteem. Of course I acted a role of confidence. I pretended that everything was okay. I wore the mask of success — but deep within myself, I was always waiting for the world to find out that I was a fake, that something was missing in my life.

In recovery I have discovered God's powerful gift of spirituality and I know that through my life a uniqueness exists in the world. I have the capacity to make the day better, not only for myself but also for others.

Thank You for the specialness of my life.

"To treat your facts with imagination is one thing,
but to imagine your facts is another."

John Burroughs

W hen I was drinking, I was always confusing
fantasy with reality. Lies got mingled with the facts
and the facts became exaggerated. It was almost
impossible for me to distinguish between reality
and fantasy, imagination and fact. My life was a
complicated lie.

Today I have a program of rigorous honesty; I must
be rigorous and stop the game before it starts. I
need to practice the principles of recovery in every
area of my life. The spiritual road involves a
comprehensive journey and nothing need be left
out.

God, who created the mountains, help me to take
responsibility for the grit between my toes.

58

"He that is without sin amongst you, let him cast the first stone."

Jesus Christ

It is so easy for me to focus on the failings of others and miss my own. My attraction to gossip is that it is usually about other people and that keeps the attention away from me. Sometimes I am made to feel good by exposing the weaknesses of others.

This attitude needs to be changed if I am ever to fully enjoy the fruits of sobriety. I do not need to be drinking to behave like a drunk; gossip and character assassination are reminiscent of my past addictive behavior. I do not need the side of me that seeks to destroy the character of others. With my spiritual program, I am trying to change.

May I grow in my forgiveness and acceptance of others.

*"Nothing stays the same. When you think you've
got something down, it changes!"*

Leo Booth

T oday I am aware that life is about change and
even the familiar, at some point in the future,
transforms.

When I was drinking, I hated change. I wanted to
control everything and everyone; things had to be
my way. Naturally, if you had asked me if I needed
to be in charge, I would have replied, "Certainly
not!" The addict's disease is fed by illusion and
denial.

Today I take a leap of faith and trust that the
Universe will still be around in the morning, and it
will probably look much the same. Today I try to
accept, one day at a time, that variety really is the
spice of life and that must include the awkward
ingredient of change.

*Creator, I accept and welcome the spiritual
ingredient of change in my life.*

Forgiveness
is the key
to action
and
freedom.

Hannah Arendt

"Understanding is the reward of faith. Therefore seek not to understand that thou mayest believe, but believe that thou mayest understand."

Saint Augustine

T oday I understand that God is love and that it makes more sense to live my life with love than with anger, resentment and despair. I know that the answer to life, with all the problems that may arise, is love. Not simply loving those people who love me, but beginning to love and understand those who dislike or hate me. Being imperfect people in an imperfect world produces enemies. Today I love my world by listening to my critics, changing unreasonable attitudes, growing in the humility that comes from silence. Change is part of God's blessing of love.

This I believe. This I understand. And step by step it is beginning to work in my life.

May my love for the world give me an understanding of self.

*"Men of integrity, by their very existence, rekindle
the belief that as a people we can live above the
level of moral squalor."*

John Gardner

I understand integrity to be a willingness to make
sacrifices for what we believe to be true. The living
of a spiritual program must lead to integrity.

Not so many years ago integrity was not an
understood word in my vocabulary because of my
unwillingness to make sacrifices. I was so selfishly
preoccupied with my wants that I gave little thought
to the needs of others. The more I lost myself in
self, the greater was the emotional pain.

Today I live the paradox that it is only in giving that
I truly receive.

*May I daily express the paradox of sacrifice
in my life.*

"The principal mark of genius is not perfection but originality, the opening of new frontiers."

Arthur Koestler

I need to remember that genius is often simplicity itself. The original thought need not be abstract, intellectual or technical; the thought exists to transmit the message.

In the slogans "Keep it Simple", "One Day at a Time", and "Don't Pick up the First Drink", wisdom combines with simplicity to produce sobriety. God is at work outside of the church and the spiritual message always brings healing. A.A. is more than a "fellowship of genius", it is divinity set to a program. What began with a group of alcoholics will cross new frontiers into the healing of the world.

Lord of Truth, let us always be open and receptive to Your voice.

"The hottest places in Hell are reserved for those, who in time of great moral crises, maintain their neutrality."

Dante Alighieri

Each human being makes a personal hell here on earth. Often we do it not by what we perpetrate but in what we allow to happen. So much of the loneliness and isolation that many addicts and their families experience is caused by them remaining hidden and silent. The pretense that everything is okay is not only untrue but deadly. Silence and compliance kills more addicts than a thousand needles!

Today I choose not to be neutral in my life. I speak about my alcoholism so that I can on a daily basis make war on the disease that nearly killed me. I speak out about the disease of addiction so that society cannot say that it did not know what was happening. I speak up for treatment and recovery because I know it can work in the vast majority of cases. I am not neutral when it comes to addiction because I am fighting for my life.

God, give me the courage to speak up in the crowd; let me live the message I was privileged to receive.

"Without freedom, no one really has a name."
Milton Acorda

P art of my identity involves my disease. I am an alcoholic and my name is ... And with this recognition of who I am comes the liberty and freedom to live and create in God's world. Who I am involves what I am; in the fusion of the two is my spiritual identity.

For years I ran from myself because I wanted to be different. I felt that I would not be acceptable or good enough for you. In running from me, I lost my identity; the seed of low self--esteem was sown.

With the spiritual recognition that I can only be who I am came the freedom of existence and identity. I am what I am!

Lord, You said once, "I am who I am."
Well, so am I!

"Hypocrisy: prejudice with a halo."

Ambrose Bierce

As a religious person I could be such a hypocrite. I thought that my goodness was dependent upon my judging others to be inferior. I was always putting other people down so that I could appear terrific.

But a part of me always knew this was wrong. I ignored the religious teaching that emphasized forgiveness and acceptance and instead focused on judgment and condemnation. It was all part of my sickness. Inside I was hurting and feeling guilty but I hid these feelings with a mask of hypocrisy and respectability.

Today I do not need to do this. I have a religion that can accept the non--religious and rejoice in the different cultures and creeds. I do not fear those who are different, and I am slowly beginning to accept my many imperfections.

You, who have loved me through forgiveness,
help me to forgive.

"An idealist is one who, on noticing that a rose smells better than a cabbage, concludes that it will also make better soup."

H.L. Mencken

The spiritual program teaches me to be an idealist with my feet on the ground. People will continue to hurt, get angry and tell lies; wrestling with imperfections is not just my problem. I need to accept that I live in an imperfect world and recovery involves reality, not illusion.

My responsibility in recovery is for my life. I cannot change other people, events or relationships; I can only change me. I am not God. Each time I forget this fact, I risk another hurt.

Help me to aspire for ideals that are within my grasp.

"Sixty years ago I knew everything; now I know nothing; education is a progressive discovery of our own ignorance."

Will Durant

Spirituality is the art of knowing that we do not know. It is waking up in the morning with our eyes fully opened and awaiting the adventure of the new day. New things, new theories, new facts are being discovered every day and it makes for a glorious, confusing and exciting world.

There was a time when I could not say this; a time when knowledge and facts were collected and regurgitated. I used knowledge to protect myself from the challenge and inconsistencies of life. God had to be not only a proven fact but evidenced in theories and dogmas — the mystery was lost.

Today I believe that God cannot be contained by dogma and rules. The doubts have become part of my faith. The state of not knowing becomes creative and stimulating. My relationship with God today is real. To not know is the beginning of wisdom.

You, who have spoken through the wind and the fire, speak through my doubts.

> *"Not he who has little, but he who wishes*
> *more, is poor."*
>
> *Seneca (4 B. C. — A. D. 65)*

In my recovery I must still deal with that compulsive side of my nature that always wants more.

I forget to be grateful for what I have. I ruin relationships because I have a code of behavior that I expect from others but not myself! I miss the fun of the moment because I am preoccupied with what I am missing elsewhere. I miss the comfort of my own home as I fantasize about country mansions owned by millionaires. Always I want more — and yet in my own experience more has always been less.

Today I work hard on a spiritual program of gratitude. I have a checklist of things I need to be grateful for; I work on my disease of greed by talking about it.

Thank You for that part of me that must
remain poor.

"We have to live today by what truth we can get today and be ready tomorrow to call it falsehood."

William James

To change is to be imperfect and to be imperfect is to be wrong — at times! As an alcoholic I have a problem with ego; always wanting to be right, hating to say, "I am sorry", not wishing to appear out of control. In sobriety I must wrestle with my ego on a daily basis.

However, although I find it difficult to accept that I am imperfect, I know that I am! I know that I need to make amends. I know that I produce most of the pain in my life. Today's facts are stepping stones to tomorrow's falsehoods — and I grow with this knowledge.

Spirituality is growing in the knowledge that I do not have all the answers.

Let me experience joy and growth in the dilemmas of life.

71

*"In freeing people ...our country's blessing will
also come; for profit follows righteousness."*

Senator Albert Beveridge

P rofit is more than financial benefit or material
well--being. Profit, for the recovering alcoholic and
drug addict, is being aware of life, feeling feelings
and having the capacity for a relationship with God,
self and others.

But a financial benefit is also part of spirituality; the
blessing of money and financial stability are part of
God's love and trust. This gift of freedom involves
our responsibility and stewardship of money.

With money and profit we are not only able to have
creative comforts, but we can also make the lives of
others creative. A responsible use of money is part
of my recovery program and has become one of the
joys of the "spiritual awakening".

*Let Your blessing of money in life help me to
bless others.*

"I have learned this at least by my experiment: that if one advances confidently in the direction of his dreams and endeavors to live the life which he has imagined, he will meet with a success unexpected in common hours."

Henry David Thoreau

Drugs brought me nightmares, never dreams. For years I lived in fear. In the night I imagined horrible shapes, strange colors and sounds, experienced unspeakable tortures and awoke in tension and sweat.

Today in sobriety my dreams are serene and tranquil; I remember friends and loved ones and those I most admire. I imagine God in the beauty of creation. God breathes love through me. My dreams are part of my wellness.

God, who created people to dream their dreams, help me to live mine.

*"There are two ways to slide easily through life:
To believe everything or to doubt everything. Both
ways save us from thinking."*

Alfred Korzybski

T his statement is so true for me. I was so
compulsive and obsessive not only about the things
that I believed in but also about the things I didn't
believe in. I was extreme. Everything I did was
exaggerated. I either raced through life at ten
thousand miles an hour or was in neutral. Balance
was absent.

Today I am developing balance in my life, more
patience and more tolerance. I have discovered that
my extremism was a mask by which I hid from life; I
did not have to think, consider or ponder — I
simply reacted.

Now I know that to believe in everything is to
believe nothing; and to doubt everything is not to
think. Life is "a many splendored thing" but it has a
variety of options.

*God of the many, help me to discover You in the
myriad of thoughts that life produces.*

"Wine that maketh glad the heart of man."

Psalm 104:15

Every good thing can be abused and alcohol is no exception. Although most people are able to enjoy the fruits of the grape and the quality of their lives are enriched by good wine, not a few are destroyed by wine! Millions of people in this world are alcoholic. They did not want to be alcoholic but they are. Their lives and relationships are destroyed by alcohol. They need to stop drinking if they are to find gladness in their lives. Alcoholism is a disease that cannot be cured, but it can be arrested by giving up the grape!

God can be appreciated in the grape, and can also be experienced in the soda. We need to find new ways to be happy.

Thank You for the precious gift of choice.

"By thought I embrace the universal."

Blaise Pascal

My ability to think and communicate enables me not only to live in this world, but also to understand this world. Relationships are dependent upon me understanding my responsibilities — and when I do not think, I am usually very irresponsible.

Alcohol stopped me from thinking and behaving responsibly and created dishonesty in my life. Instead of feeling I belonged, I felt I was on the outside; instead of enjoying relationships, I was forever fighting and involved in bitter disputes; instead of enjoying the peace that comes from being a child of God, I felt like an abandoned creature. My problem was alcohol, and I needed to do something about it.

I did — I stopped taking the first drink. Today I am alive in my life, alive in God's world and enjoying this universe.

When I think clearly, I know I belong.

> *"A free society is one where it is safe*
> *to be unpopular."*
>
> *Adlai Stevenson*

Tough love requires that at times I must say or do things that make me unpopular. That is part of the spiritual risk of loving: to be popular is not always to be right!

As an alcoholic I was a people--pleaser; concerned with saying what people wanted to hear, do what people expected, remain silent rather than cause upsets. I was afraid that if I said what I really thought, I might be rejected. My self--esteem was secondary to what other people thought of me.

Today in my sobriety I love myself enough to say what I believe and do what I consider right. I refuse to remain silent when confronted with injustice or the addictions of others. My spiritual program risks the possibility of being unpopular.

Teach me to always say and do what I believe to be true.

"The saints are the sinners who keep on going."
Robert Louis Stevenson

At times I do not want to carry on; I do not want to fight anymore for truth and freedom; it seems so much easier to "give up" and agree with everybody — but I know, deep inside myself, this is not true.

At times the disease speaks to me and tells me to give up and everything will be okay — perhaps have one drink, don't rush off to so many meetings, get what you can when you can! It all sounds so tempting, but I know that it does not work.

Sobriety works! The struggle and pain to act responsibly in my life is paying off and it does get better. I am not going to give up. My life is worth more than a quick fix!

Lord, let me know that true courage is working through the pain.

*"Humor may be defined as the kindly
contemplation of the incongruities of life and the
artistic impression thereof ... The essence of humor
is human kindliness."*

Stephen Leacock

Humor for me is a key to balance. In the joke I am able to release some tension or frustration and cope with my disease of alcoholism. When I drank, I did not have a genuine sense of humor — rather it was sarcasm, cruel put--downs or insane expressions of my manic personality. My fun was created at the expense of others. It was a form of violence. It kept people away from me and created a loneliness in my life.

Today I seek to use humor as an expression of acceptance, tolerance, understanding and forgiveness. Humor is an aspect of my spiritual program. In humor I experience God.

*Give me the gift of humor that reflects the dignity
and hope for us all.*

"Sanity is madness put to good use."

George Santayana

I heard the phrase "make the disease work for you". It made a great deal of sense to me and still does. I am a recovering alcoholic. My alcoholism is still within me and every day I take the necessary steps to stay sober. My disease is that "mad" part of me that wants to destroy my life, relationships and understanding of God. What I need to do is accept my "madness" and turn it around so that it works for me. My suffering is the key to my spiritual growth. My anger and manipulation helps me to understand the imperfections of others. My powerlessness over alcohol give me an understanding of humility that is based on reality. The acceptance of my "madness" keeps me sane!

O God, give me the sanity to accept my imperfections so that I can grow into the best that I can be.

> *"Science may have found a cure for most evils; but it has found no remedy for the worst of them all — the apathy of human beings."*
>
> *Helen Keller*

I read today of a woman who ate herself to death. Friends and family when interviewed said, "She simply didn't seem to care." She had stuffed her feelings for so long that she had forgotten what they were; she had lost her spirituality. Apathy kills people.

So long as people do nothing, the disease of addiction gets worse and more victims are claimed. Apathy feeds ignorance because it stops activity; apathy stops life.

The antidote for apathy is spirituality. Spiritual people are alive with positive attitudes and creative hope — and they are infectious. People are challenged to discover a meaning to life in their own lives. Hope produces recovery; recovery produces a message that must be shared; in the message is the miracle of life.

I pray that in the face of apathy I can discover hope.

"I love my country better than my family; but I love humanity better than my country."

Francois Fenelon

W e need to think big. We need to escape from those little concepts that keep us small. Life is more than we can ever perceive. We need to see it in its totality. The nuclear family can be restrictive if taken as the center of our loyalty. Even our national citizenship needs to be placed in the context of the world. Our freedom rests in our universal humanity.

Spirituality is about thinking big. It is finding God in the richness of creation. Our insistence on our shared humanity is the path to world peace and serenity. Divisions should not exist for the humanitarian who seeks acceptance for all individuals simply because they are people.

May I seek to find the One in the many — and the many in the One.

"God will forgive me; that's his business."

Heinrich Heine

It took me a long time to accept that God had forgiven the deeds done in my addiction. It took me a long time to comprehend that God is forgiveness, "forgiving love". Forgiveness unites us with God because it is God's nature to forgive.

When I am living the spiritual life, I can unite myself with God by my acts of forgiveness. And when I forgive others, I am doing a kindness, an act of forgiveness, to myself. Hate used to drain me of energy and it still can if I get caught up in resentments. Forgiveness restores energy and peace.

When I forgive, I am at one with God.

In the forgiveness of others I discover me.

"No matter how old you get, if you keep the desire to be creative, you're keeping the man--child alive."

John Cassavetes

When I was a child, I used to play in the sand and make castles. I would build a strong and firm fortress around the castle so that it could withstand the force of the sea.

Today I also like to play in my life and I need to build strong and firm behavioral structures that will withstand pressure and stress. Today I need to build my life on a sure foundation — and that foundation must be me! I need to take care of me so that I can enjoy my life.

How do I take care of me? I watch what I drink. I am a recovering alcoholic, and so I choose not to drink alcohol. I drink soda, orange juice and milk — but no alcohol. This is an important part of my self--love program. I exercise regularly. I watch what I eat and I avoid sugar and needless carbohydrates. I rest in the evenings and take walks in the fresh air. The child that is in me still lives, but today he is healthy.

Help me to treat life responsibly, but not too seriously.

"Language is the light of the mind."

John Stuart Mill

W hen I was drinking, I never really thought about how I behaved, how I dressed or the language I used. Today I believe I should be responsible for the whole of me.

Language is important because it is my bridge to others; it is also the vehicle for understanding the ideas of others. Spirituality involves the concept of language because it is the means of growth, communication and relationship. My words help me to be known. My ability to understand the ideas and aspirations of others helps me to feel that I belong.

God is perceived in this world and the gift of language is one of the ways God is revealed. My words are spiritual.

May the light of God's eternal truth be manifested in the way I talk and relate to others.

> *"I know of no more encouraging fact than the unquestionable ability of man to elevate his life by a conscious endeavor."*
>
> *Henry David Thoreau*

Life is exciting to me when I am creating, when I am pursuing a dream, when I am making miracles in my life.

I suppose perseverance stems from a belief that things get better when we roll up our sleeves and do something. Sobriety is about comprehending that in our lives we reflect the message.

God has created humanity with the ability to make the dream come true; this is not to say it is easy … but it is harder not to dream!

Teach us to wonder at the stars with a spade in our hands.

> *"The art of teaching is the art of*
> *assisting discovery."*
>
> *Mark Van Doren*

I need a "sponsor" in my life. Somebody I turn to when I have problems, when I am confused or in pain, when I simply need to talk, when I feel lonely or when I am about to make a major change in my life. Addicts like me need a sponsor; somebody to bounce ideas off, especially ideas that affect the living of my life because I truly understand that the disease of alcoholism lives in my life!

My sponsor guides, suggests and gently leads me to where I need to go; he does not demand or dictate. My sponsor is a friend whom I can trust, and he makes a point of not being a fixer in my life. He will not allow me to escape into his life. He will not allow me to become addicted to him.

O God, let me always be free enough to discover You
in my life.

"It is all one to me if a man comes from Sing Sing or Harvard. We hire a man not his history."

Henry Ford

So often we can get so locked into our history -- what we did, what we said, the events of which we were ashamed -- that we miss the gift of the new day.

Those of us who suffer from the disease of addiction need to deal with past problems but not live in them. Our attitude towards today need not be based on what happened yesterday. Today is the beginning of the rest of our lives. Today I know that I create most of the pain and tragedy in my life, but I also know that I create the joys and successes. I am confident that my sobriety makes me a winner.

Lord, I forgive myself for yesterday and look forward to the healing that comes with today.

*"The future is hidden even from the men
who made it."*

Anatole France

Life is a glorious mystery. We can never fully understand it and it will always confuse and amaze us. After we have understood one thing, we are presented with a fresh problem. We are not perfect. We are not God. We will never understand completely.

Some years ago this used to anger and irritate me. I wanted to know everything. I wanted to have the answer to all life's problems. I wanted the power that comes with perfection. I hated being vulnerable, weak and confused! I hated being human. Yes, that was my problem. I hated being a human being.

Today I am enjoying the adventure of life, and I kneel in awe at its mingled complexity. Today life is a paradox that I can live with.

Help me to accept the mystery of life.

"Opinions cannot survive if one has no chance to fight for them."

Thomas Mann

An opinion is worth fighting for, and I have opinions on a great number of subjects -- as a result of sobriety.

Drugs have a tendency to make insane remarks appear brilliant; drunks always see themselves as unsung poets or victimized geniuses when they are "in alcohol". I did not have opinions when I was drinking but rather a series of chaotic and incoherent reactions.

But today I have considered opinions. I am able to think and make decisions. I am able to make a contribution to life and the world in which I live. I am involved.

More than this, today I have the spiritual confidence to fight for what I believe and speak out my concerns in love. Today I am alive and I love it -- also I love me.

Let me always hear the opinions of others but not fail to express my own.

"For here we are not afraid to follow wherever it may lead, nor to tolerate error so long as reason is free to combat it."

Thomas Jefferson

As an alcoholic I was so often afraid to challenge the thinking and ideas of other people. My people pleasing demanded peace at any price. And yet so much of what I heard, read and practiced I did not agree with. Now I see that my behavior, my attitude — along with the alcohol consumption — kept me sick.

In my spiritual program today I am free to reject, consider and have my own opinions in life. I do not simply have to agree with everything that is said, in this way I am discovering my value and self-esteem.

Lord, I am grateful for the freedom to cooperate.

> *"All wars are civil wars, because all men are brothers ...Each one owes infinitely more to the human race than to the particular country in which he was born."*
>
> *Francois Fenelon*

My disease of addiction kept me separate, isolated and alone. I was so busy seeing how I was different from other people that I missed the similarities. I missed the "oneness" of this creation by always placing myself above it, below it, outside it: and I was the loser.

Even my religion kept me separate. I was a Christian and not a Jew, Muslim or Hindu — but I failed to see the similarities of these major philosophies; I failed to see what all religious people have in common; I failed to see the inclusiveness of Love, Truth and Forgiveness.

God is to be found in both the difference and sameness of all people.

> *O Lord, I am discovering that even the differences, when understood, become the same.*

"I would I could stand on a busy corner, hat in
hand, and beg people throw me their
wasted hours."

Bernard Berenson

I enjoy my sobriety so much that I hate to waste my time. Part of my spiritual program involves a correct use of time. I will not spend time with negative or destructive people. I will not spend time in useless gossip or doing things I do not enjoy to please other people.

I am enjoying life so much I do not wish to waste any of it. Spirituality involves a creative stewardship of time.

As an alcoholic I wasted so much time. For most of my life I was "out to lunch"! Today I spend time enjoying my life — and I spend quality time alone with "self". I enjoy my little conversations with self — the thoughts I have and need to ponder upon. I need time to rest in the peace of my life. Time is a precious gift from God that should not be wasted.

Lord, let me live each day as if it were my last.

> *"The real problem is in the hearts and*
> *minds of men."*
>
> *Albert Einstein*

We are facing not so much a "drug problem" as a "people problem" — and this requires a solution from the people. I believe the solution and recovery has already been given by God, but it must be discovered from within. We need to seek out what is truly in our minds and hearts: what are our problems, what are our needs, what do we long for, where are we going in our lives?

Today it is not enough for me to know my problems, I need also to talk about them. Today I choose to express my feelings.

> *God, I thank You for the creative gift of*
> *communication.*

"Men love to wonder, and that is the seed of science"

Ralph Waldo Emerson

In my sobriety the world is a wonderful place. I often sit back and am amazed at the splendor of life, at the simple happenings that give such joy, at the nobility that is revealed in man, at the creative adventure and mystery of life. I meditate in wonder.

Now I see how drugs kept me blind from so much. Alcohol kept me a prisoner of mediocrity and much of the wonder of life passed me by. As a drinking alcoholic I existed in life, rather than lived life. I was a bored spectator rather than a participant. I reacted to things, rather than initiated events Alcoholism equals dullness. Recovery symbolized energy.

Today I can dream dreams and rest in the wonder of it all. God is Good.

O Lord, let me see the wonderful mystery of life even in the ordinary.

"Beauty is not caused. It is."

Emily Dickinson

So many people think that beauty is what you do to yourself; what you wear, makeup, clothes, hairstyles or expensive jewelry. Again it is so easy to get caught up in things. Reality is not about what we wear but who we are.

The beauty that God has created comes from within. The twinkle in the eyes that says "hello". The hug that says "I love you". The gentle embrace and smile that says "I forgive you". The tear that cries " I understand".

When God said to the world, "It is good", Beauty was born. Drugs and crazy relationships only get in the way of us being what we were intended to be: beautiful for God.

Today I seek to put God's beauty in my actions, words and attitudes.

"No man is a failure who is enjoying life."
William Feather

S pirituality is fun. I enjoy my sobriety today and I do not take myself too seriously.

For years I thought I was a failure and this thought manifested the behavior of a failure. I hid, sulked, was jealous, carried resentments and isolated myself from life — and then blamed the world.

Today because I really understand and accept that I am a child of God, I know that I am not a failure and I have a glorious future in recovery. Today I have hope. Today I have confidence. Today I am able to accept and forgive. Today I am able to love my neighbor because I love myself.

In my enjoyment of life may I reflect your love for the world.

"Though pride is not a virtue, it is the parent of many virtues."

M. C. Collins

I need to remember that pride is not necessarily a negative. It is sensible to have a balanced pride in my sobriety because self--esteem will grow from the pride and respect I give to myself. God has made me and is involved with me and, therefore, I am a beautiful person.

Balanced pride helps me with my appearance, grooming and personal etiquette that comes with clothes, fashion and hairstyles. Pride helps me with my communication skills — I work hard at being understood, speaking out clearly and developing better methods of being understood.

Pride stops me from being taken advantage of, enabling me to say no to others while still feeling good about myself. A healthy sense of pride is essential for spiritual growth.

Lord, let me have a realistic appreciation of myself that leads to achievement.

"You just wake up one morning and you got it!"
Moms Mabley

I am so busy living I don't think about getting old. I am so grateful in my recovery from alcoholism that tomorrow, the future and age are secondary.

In my sickness I was always living in the future; what would tomorrow bring? Will I die crippled, lonely and afraid? My projections into the future produced an emotional pain.

Today I do not need to do this. I welcome old age because I bring into it the joy and experience of my sobriety. Will I be lonely? I doubt it if I stick to my recovery program; I have so many friends all over the world meeting together to face the disease on a daily basis. Also I know that nothing could ever compare with the loneliness of my drinking days.

My spiritual program reminds me to be grateful for my life and this includes the inevitability of old age.

Lord, as I grow in age may I also grow in wisdom and tolerance.

*"It takes a wise man to handle a lie; a fool had
better remain honest."*

Norman Douglas

As a drinking alcoholic I was telling so many lies
to cover the lies I had previously told that I got lost
in a maze of untruth! Most of the lies were stupid,
irrelevant and harmless — but they were all aimed
at building up my ego. Making me look good.
Telling people I had more. My memory could not
keep up with my tongue and I became guilty,
ashamed and embarrassed.

Today I need to remember that there is nothing any
lie can give me that I need; there is nothing in the
world of fabrication that I need; I have what I need.

Today I have a relationship with a God and Friend
that I can understand and be vulnerable with; I
don't need to be perfect to be loved.

*Help me to seek the good life in those things that are
good.*

"No one is useless in this world who lightens the burdens of another."

Charles Dickens

As a drunk I thought that the world owed me a living. Everybody existed for my employment and service; the world was waiting for my telephone call! For years I manipulated people, and I was such a good con artist they often left thanking me!

Today a part of my spiritual program requires service. I make the coffee, put out the cookies, cook the meal and invite friends for dinner. I make the telephone call, give the lectures, share in groups and write articles. The life of service helps to keep me sober. I am the message that I share. And I do it for me!

Thank You for making me aware of my need to give.

"Real generosity towards the future consists in giving all to what is present."

Albert Camus

Much of the gratitude that I talk about needs to be centered in what I do with today; I need to focus on the present, rather than procrastinate for the future.

As a sick alcoholic I lived either in the guilt of yesterday or the fear of tomorrow — missing the reality of the present. The present moment is all that I have and through this "moment" I live and breathe and have my existence!

My understanding of prayer is centered in the present moment because any understanding of relationship and communication, especially with God, must begin from where one is, rather than where one would like to be. Spirituality is the reality of the moment.

Lord, thank You for the life that is experienced in the moment.

*"Nothing can bring you peace but the triumph
of principles."*

Ralph Waldo Emerson

Slowly I am understanding what principles are in
my life. I am learning to live with a code of ethics
that I do not always like, but I know is good for me
and others. Although I do not always fully
understand the spiritual principles of life, I know
that my ongoing recovery should be based upon
them.

Some of the spiritual principles by which I try to live
are: Honesty, Truth, Openness, Forgiveness,
Acceptance, Humility and Hope.

I am also experiencing a personal satisfaction in
knowing that I am living today with a set of
principles that work. They enable me to be a feeling
and loving human being. Today I am beginning to
feel what I always thought other people had. Today
I am alive in my life.

May Your principles be my lifestyle.

103

> *"Every man, on the foundation of his own*
> *sufferings and joys, builds for all."*
>
> *Albert Camus*

In my pain I am able to reach out to others. When I share my pain, I not only understand but I am understood. It is my pain and suffering that unites me with others. Other people become a part of my life and are involved in who I am.

Through my shared feelings, other people begin to share. Trust develops across this bridge of understanding. Feelings unite the world.

Lord, You created us in ONENESS — help us in our struggle to unite.

"I tend to be suspicious of people whose love of animals is exaggerated; they are often frustrated in their relationship with humans."

Yila (Camilla Koffler)

Anything can be used to avoid dealing with reality. People can use alcohol, food, drugs, people, sex, gambling — and yes, even animals — to avoid dealing with their loneliness and feelings of isolation.

The key to addiction is to be found in the obsessive and compulsive behavior patterns that stop us from reaching our full potential as human beings. We cannot relax with who we are because of our exaggerated and painful lifestyles. We cannot truly love ourselves because of our obsession with the "it" that seems to be controlling us. At some point we need to see the obsession and begin to talk about it.

In order for me to be a spiritual person I must free myself from compulsive attitudes.

God, I meditate on the comfortableness of freedom.

"May you live all the days of your life."

Jonathan Swift

I heard a story that offers a key to the meaning of spirituality:

Two little fish were huddled together, afraid to move. A large fish swam by them, confident and strong. The big fish shouted out to the two little fish, "Why don't you swim out and enjoy the beautiful ocean?" The two little fish looked at each other and asked, "Where is the ocean?" They were in it but they didn't know it!

As an alcoholic I existed in life but I didn't live: I missed vacations, people, friendships, feelings, nature, sunsets and God. Like so many addicts, I was numbered amongst the "walking dead". Today I continue to make a spiritual choice that avoids alcohol and I am able to feel again. Today I am alive.

In You I live to love and love to live.

"People who take time to be alone usually have depth, originality and quiet reserve."

John Miller

I need to be alone. I need time to listen to my thoughts, consider my opinions and strengthen my body. I need to pull away from my hectic life to be alone with me.

As a drinking alcoholic I hated to be alone. I became paranoiac about "leaving the fort" — today I accept that nobody is indispensable and that the world will still be there when I return from the desert!

Today I grow in the stillness of solitude. I can rest in that "still" part of me that is the essential me.

God is very close to me in the silence of self.

Lord, in the stillness of Your life, I am healed and rejuvenated.

*"You grow up the day you have the first real laugh
— at yourself."*

Ethel Barrymore

Today I can laugh at myself. I do not take myself
too seriously and I am beginning to grow. I used to
be so serious. Having the "poor me's", sitting on my
pity pot demanding attention, I was so unhappy.
And I was causing my unhappiness.

Then a friend listened to my complaints for half an
hour and then began to laugh, giving out a real
belly--laugh and at that point I began to laugh, too!
My attitude was so stupid, selfish and futile that it
demanded a laugh to shake me out of it — at that
point I began to grow.

Today I laugh at my funny little ways, my funny
little walk, my ridiculous pretensions, my grandiose
behavior. Today with the laughter comes humility.

O Lord, let me experience the miracle of laughter.

"Power does not corrupt. Fear corrupts, perhaps the fear of loss of power."

John Steinbeck

In my recovery I am beginning to understand that so much power in the world is really fear. The power that seeks to attack first in order to feel secure is really fear. The power that always has to have an answer is really fear. The power that arrogantly refuses to listen is really fear. So much power is fear dressed in illusion!

Spiritual power has the ability to be vulnerable. It can live with confusion. It can stand alone. It allows others to walk away to pursue their happiness. Spiritual power can exist in suffering and loneliness, and it does not expect perfection.

My recovery is teaching me to live and let others live, too. My freedom must respect the freedom of others; respect is a two--way street!

Give me the power that can rest in imperfection.

"Any God I ever felt in Church I brought in with me. And I think all the other folks did, too. They come to Church to share God, not find God."

Alice Walker

God is within us! At one time I would find that statement blasphemous or incomprehensible. I always thought God was a long way off — separate, unknowable and judgmental. God was much more a judge than a friend. I saw myself more the sinner than the son. Naturally, with such a low self--esteem it was hard to associate God with my life, let alone consider God existing within me!

Then I began to search for the spiritual path that leads to a deeper understanding of self. I found a loving, gentle and friendly God whose love was so pervasive in the world that I was able to discover God in my life and the lives of others. The concept of meeting together to share God made sense. The concept of discovering a God within and without made God knowable and comprehensible. Because God lives in me, I am alive.

God, in the breaking of the bread, may I share Your life in my world.

*"Freedom is the right to choose: the right to create
for yourself the alternatives of choice. Without the
possibility of choice and the exercise of choice a
man is not a man but a member, an instrument,
a thing ..."*

Archibald MacLeish

Spirituality involves the freedom to change; it
requires the variety of choice in order to grow.

My past addiction was a life of slavery because it
removed from me creative choice and left me
obsessing about drugs and alcohol. My life,
conversation and thoughts revolved around the
bottle, and I was oblivious to the true meaning of
life. I could not do better in my life because I was
addicted not only to drugs but to the destructive
lifestyle that goes with them. My freedom to
experience the spiritual power of God's creativity
was lost to a mindless craving for drugs; in this
sense, drug addiction is slavery.

Today I am free to see God's world in people,
places and things and I make a choice to live, love
and laugh.

*I am growing in the awareness of Your multifaceted
love for me.*

111

"There is nothing permanent except change."

Heraclitus

Today I know that I need to change. I accept that my behavior and attitude were negative and destructive. Today I make a choice to work on my addiction. I was changing before I embraced a spiritual program but the change was for the worse. Each day I grew more dependent, more isolated, more angry and depressed. I felt I was a hopeless case!

Today I am working on my anger and loneliness. I talk about those things that cause me pain and distress. I express my fears and resentments — and it is getting better.

God created this world in perpetual change and I believe that God is to be discovered in the change. I am evolving into Truth with my small steps towards recovery. The steps I take towards recovery are my "yes" to God.

In the daily changes I discover the stability of God.

*"A man who dares to waste one hour of time has
not discovered the value of life."*

Charles Darwin

Life is not to be wasted. Time is not to be
wasted. Friends, relationships, opportunities are
not to be wasted. Why? Because as vulnerable
human beings we do not have the ultimate control
of our lives and none of us know when our lives will
end, when we shall die, when time and opportunity
will be no more! Life is too precious to waste.

During my years as an addict I did not value my life.
I did not value time. I did not value friends and
relationships. Nothing was valued except the
alcohol! Life was meaningless. God was absent and
I felt nothing — just a dullness at the center of my
being. Today this is not the case. Through my pain I
have found the value of life and I have discovered a
God of my understanding.

God, let me value what I have while I have it.

"I have my own particular sorrows, loves, delights; and you have yours. But sorrow, gladness, yearning, hope, love belong to all of us, in all times and in all places. Music is the only means whereby we feel these emotions in their universality."

H. A. Overstreet

A language for the world is music. It unites all peoples, cultures, religions and backgrounds; it points people beyond themselves, while at the same time breathing through them God's glory. Music makes people wonder, enables them to dream, allows them to rest in the miracle of creativity.

Drugs stopped me from appreciating the gift of music. They twisted and corrupted sounds and made them destructive and coarse. Drugs took from me so much and left me with a feeling of utter emptiness.

In my recovery I can hear again. My spiritual program incorporates music, different types of music, the inexhaustible joys of melody. I can feel in it, through it, with it — another miracle.

Thank You for the gift of music that enables me to grow in my understanding of self and my need of others.

"To say that a man is made up of certain chemical elements is a satisfactory description only for those who intend to use him as a fertilizer."

Herbert J. Muller

Humans are more than chemicals. A person is more than an animal. Human beings carry the image of God, the imprint of Divinity, the power of the creative God.

As an addict I doubted myself, only adding to my powerlessness and unmanageability. Internally, I said, "I can't" before I tried. My low self--esteem was evident long before I took a drink. I was always trying to get my "outsides" to match what I imagined your "insides" to be like.

When I accepted my alcoholism I was able to discover God in my life. Today I am able to create through God and in God. Spirituality comes with the awareness of our God--given divinity.

May I never cease to see You in my life.

"Man is what he believes."

Anton Chekhov

My miracle is that I now believe in me. Today I accept my disease of addiction and I do not resist or deny it. I believe that I am an alcoholic. I believe that I am an overeater. I am a co--dependent. I believe that I am an adult child of an alcoholic. And this belief enables me to be free.

For too long I played the game of control, blaming and bargaining — and I lost. Now I choose to surrender to the reality of who I am. I accept my disease on a daily basis and I make choices with the awareness of my disease. And it is getting better.

My belief about my addiction has also given me an insight into God and God's gift of freedom. God loves me enough to give me choice and with this gift comes responsibility. I believe that I am responsible for how I live with my addictions. Today I accept that responsibility.

What I believe reflects the God I believe in; I believe in Freedom.

"In the country of the blind the one-eyed king can still goof up."

Anonymous

For years I tried to control everything and everybody. Things had their place; there was a correct code of behavior for doing things; everything had to have its place. I felt responsible for the universe and everybody in it.

Today I can laugh at my mistakes and the mistakes of others. When I catch myself organizing the world, I remember where the "perfect" yesterdays got me — and I laugh. God made me with a navel and flat feet; I would have preferred something different but there is a loving message within my imperfections: It is okay to goof up!

Today I relax in the humor of being human. Thank You for making me an angel in the dirt.

"If the work of God could be comprehended by reason, it would be no longer wonderful, and faith would have no merit if reason provided proof."

Pope Gregory I

Some things happen that I do not understand or comprehend, but I have faith that they will happen tomorrow: sunsets, night following day, the song of the bird, the colors of nature, and the joy and adventure of being alive. Perhaps the biggest mystery for humankind to grapple with is love — a people will suffer, endure persecution, even be put to death for something they love. The pain and sorrow of love is mingled into what it is to be a human being.

Reason does not have the answer to life. Faith is the medication for our existence. We have a belief in tomorrow because of what we have experienced today. If I can say no to alcohol today then I can do it tomorrow — if I really want to.

Lord, let me not seek for proof but daily seek to grapple with the problems of life.

"All religions must be tolerated . . . for . . . every
man must get to heaven his own way."

Frederick the Great

There are many ways to God and I believe that Christianity is one way. However, I am convinced that there are other ways with or without religion. My experience of the church has been good, and I have been encouraged to question and doubt, search for new areas of faith within my agnosticism, explore other religions. My experience of Christianity has been supportive of openness and compassion.

God is not a prisoner of any religion and we can all learn from each other's experiences — but we need to listen. To dismiss arrogantly the value that a religion can bring is, to my way of thinking, as negative and sick as to accept what a religion says without question.

Let me find in the religions of the world the
ONENESS of Your truth.

"It is never too late to give up your prejudices."
Henry David Thoreau

Prejudice divides people and feeds upon anger, resentment and fear. Today I can see that my prejudices stemmed from my seeing in others what I disliked in myself. I hated people who appeared weak because I knew that I was weak and vulnerable. I hated people who were different because I knew there were parts of me that were different from how I appeared. I hated the people who stood up for their principles and talked about their feelings because, as a drunk, I never really had any principles and I couldn't get in touch with my feelings.

Today I try to talk about my prejudices and overcome them. A knowledge of those people I disliked has proven useful in slowly overcoming my prejudices.

Teach me to locate myself in my criticism of others.

"Man, unlike the animals, has never learned that the sole purpose of life is to enjoy it."

Samuel Butler

Spirituality enables me to enjoy my life. I enjoy my sobriety. I enjoy the freedom of a God of my understanding. I enjoy the fellowship of ideas and opinions that are based on love and honest sharing. The world is to be enjoyed and not endured! God is fun.

For years I thought that God was a judge to be feared; angry, hostile and revengeful. Strange how silly this all seems now, but for years I was afraid of God and feared God's presence. Then I was introduced to a God who is beyond institutions and dogmas, free of creeds and punishments, a loving and joyous God who created me to be happy. Today I am enjoying my freedom.

God, the Creatorr of the Universe, is also the parent to us all.

"Originality does not consist in saying what no one has ever said before, but in saying exactly what you think yourself."

James Stephens

Sometimes I surprise myself with what I say, think or contemplate. Within my being is a very strange world that I wish to share with others. Why? Because if I am truly honest about what I think and feel, it may unite me with the true identity of others. Perhaps we are all a little strange! However I will never know what people are thinking or feeling unless I take a risk and share my honest feelings. My involvement with my fellow humans revolves around my honesty.

In the knowledge of Your love let me share my feelings.

No man is
a failure
who
is enjoying
life.

William Feather

*"Nobody ever outgrows Scriptures; the book widens
and deepens with our years."*

Charles Haddan Spurgeon

Not so long ago I had a narrow and rigid religious outlook that was based solely on my narrow belief system. I was addicted to my religious approach and any alternative or variation was condemned before investigation. I was a religious bigot. I was a hypocrite. I hid behind my dogma and practiced ritual.

Today I have a comprehensive view of religion and God, thanks to the influence of recovering alcoholics and the discovery of a spiritual program. Today I am able to see the depth and richness of scripture, a living library of books and experiences. Today I am able to see beyond the printed word to the message of healing and love that comes with honesty and acceptance. Now I know that the bigoted side of me was fearful and afraid of change. I needed rules to keep people from discovering what a lonely and spiritually bereft person I was. The rules and dogmas formed my prison bars. I was drowning in religiosity. Today I am free to be different. Today I am free to be me.

*O wind of Truth, continue to blow and inspire us
through our differences.*

> *"Facts do not cease to exist because they*
> *are ignored."*
>
> *Aldous Huxley*

Reality is not dependent upon our acceptance. Addiction does not have to be accepted to be real. Alcoholism was killing people long before it had a name!

Ineed to remember this in the recovery program for my life. A big part of my life was spent denying that I had a problem. My manipulative art was exercised in discovering more acceptable excuses for my drunkenness, rather than looking at the problem. I danced toward death with God and denial on my lips. Belief in the God of Truth did not stop my dishonesty.

The process of self--love and acceptance began in my cry for help. Surrender brought me sanity. God's purpose was being worked out in my life because I was getting out of my way; I was facing the facts. Spirituality is making the words fit the feelings, and the feelings make the action.

Help me never to ignore what I know to be true.

125

"God sees nothing average."

Anonymous

God created every human being from the dust and and bestowed within all of us God's image. This means that we are divine. We are creatures created to create. We share God's life for the universe. We are anything but average!

And yet for years we thought we were not good enough. We needed drugs, food or people to make us okay. We considered ourselves less--than, inferior or freaks.

But today we awake to a new message. The spiritual message tells us that we are forever holding God's hand. God needs you and me to work in the divine vineyard. In us God makes miracles. Today I know that I am beautiful. I am important. I am unique.

Creator, part of Your beauty is in Your healing power. Help me to be healed daily by beholding my beauty that is forever within and without.

"War is only a cowardly escape from the problems of peace."

Thomas Mann

Sometimes it is easier to attack than it is to discuss and seek harmony. It is easier to lash out, hurt, maim or destroy than it is to listen, forgive, understand and reconcile. Violence is so often the cowardly way out.

The sadness for our society is that war and violence are often presented as manly or heroic. Our modern heroes so often carry weapons rather than the olive branch. Surrender is seen as cowardice. Gentleness is seen as weakness. The diplomat is seen as the schemer.

My recovery teaches me that nothing is gained by acts of violence, whereas in the atmosphere of peace, God and humankind can be reconciled.

Give me the courage to surrender on a daily basis and bring harmony into my world.

"Hope is the pillar that holds up the world. Hope is the dream of the working man."

Pliny the Elder

I look at the world and I discover an order, a pattern to life, a balance within the system. I do not believe in a God of chaos. I find a spiritual stability in creation. Night follows day; people, regardless of culture or creed, are remarkably similar in feelings and needs; death makes way for life. The God who created this world has given the seeds of hope within the living of life. I am the key to the understanding of the universe.

In this observation I find hope. If I continue to go with the flow of life, I will find peace and stability. It is only when I fight the system that I experience pain.

May the God of order and stability continue to bring balance into my life by the spiritual changes I continue to make.

"In every real man a child is hidden that wants to play."

Friedrich Nietzsche

My spiritual program means that I can play and have fun in my life. I am forty years old and I can still enjoy going on the swings in the park. But more importantly I have a daily sense of adventure. My eyes light up as I ask: How? When? Where? These words still dominate my life.

I can still get excited about life; I can still get excited about my life.

God is forever present in this world of color, movement and change. But for me God is most clearly seen in people. They are a constant fascination for me. Part of my play involves people--watching and as I gaze my mouth still opens in amazement. The child in me still enjoys the world in which I play.

Thank You for toys, people and difference because they add color to my life.

"There is no failure except in no longer trying."
Elbert Hubbard

I produced the failure in my life. For years I would blame everything and everyone — my parents, the job, my health, low income, a cruel world, thoughtless friends, the weather! Today I am able to own my failures because they are mine.

Today I am also able to see my successes — and this makes me a winner. I am able to see the things that I have achieved, the character defects I have confronted, the happiness that comes with an acceptance of self.

I may not be perfect but I am certainly not worthless. I may make mistakes but I am not evil. I have a heart that needs to love and also needs to be loved. Today I am able to reveal my vulnerability and discover its strength.

This underling is learning how to fly.

God, may I continue to seek Your power and glory in my life.

"Where is there dignity unless there is honesty?"

Marcus Cicero

T he cornerstone of my life today is honesty. It is the quality I most desire in my life because I believe that with honesty comes a knowledge of God, self and relationships. It is the key to my recovery from addiction. It is the key to the meaning of spirituality. Honesty affords me hope for tomorrow.

As an alcoholic I was dishonest. I was not just dishonest because I told lies and manipulated the truth, I was dishonest because I refused to risk the journey into self. My dishonesty was not about what I said but what I did not say! Not so much about what I did but what I did not do. My dishonesty stopped me from discovering my God--given dignity.

Today I risk the journey into self and I am discovering more about God as I understand God. My level of honesty helps me to be happy and relaxed with who I am today.

"Be still and know that I am God." In the silence of self--honesty may I know myself.

> *"Poetry is the rhythmical creation of*
> *beauty in words."*
>
> *Edgar Allan Poe*

Language helps us to understand and communicate. Poetry adds the dimension of "shape" and "movement". Poetry seems to go beyond words and ideas to the very essence of what life is about; it hints at divinity!

When I was drinking, I never understood the art of poetry. Today I use poetry as part of my adventure into meaning and self--knowledge.

So much more is open to me in sobriety, and I am able to appreciate things I never used to comprehend. Poetry is part of "it gets better".

Help me to seek You through all aspects of art.

"When one is painting, one does not think."

Raphael Sanzio

Artists are predominantly people who feel rather than think; they are molding their most inner experiences into the finished product.

I am doing the same in my sobriety. Today I am molding something good and wholesome from a life that was negative an destructive. I am rediscovering God, not just in thoughts and ideas, but in the daily happenings of my life. God is not only an idea but is alive in my relationships, behavior and daily acts of kindness.

God is a process in which I am involved. God is at the center of my life, regardless of the ordinariness of the event. Art is part of my life because I am a creative human being.

Teach me to look beyond the painting into myself.

"Procrastination — the art of keeping up with yesterday."

Don Marquis

Today I try to do all that I have set myself to do in a given day. I make a list of things that I need to do and a list of those thing that I want to do—the things I need to do usually take priority.

This was not always the case. As a drinking alcoholic my life was littered with promises that were never kept, intentions that were never honored, appointments and meetings that did not happen. I pushed everything into tomorrow—and tomorrow never came.

My understanding of spirituality involves a responsibility for those things that I need to do. When I awake, I thank God for my sleep and I make a silent intention not to drink today; then I face my responsibilities. I separate my "needs" from my "wants" and I remember that I have a responsibility to other people: family, friends and colleagues. Today I am learning to live in my day.

God, may I do the things I should do and may I find time for those things I want to do.

"Man must cease attributing his problems to his environment and learn again to exercise his will, his personal responsibility in the realm of faith and morals."

Albert Schweitzer

God has created me to be a responsible human being and that means that I must seriously consider the choices and decisions that could affect my life and the lives of others. Today I understand that true freedom can only be experienced within the restraints of a responsible life.

For years I blamed other people for my drunken behavior — family, bishops, job, world situations — even God! But the truth was that I lived an irresponsible life around alcohol. I ignored the facts that surrounded my drinking.

Today I make a responsible decision not to drink, and I also take responsibility for my life. I cannot blame other people for the mistakes that I made. My real freedom is experienced in my responsibility.

Give me the freedom to impose my own constraints.

"Argument is the worst sort of conversation."

Jonathan Swift

W hy did I argue so much? Why do I argue so much! Usually it is because I feel threatened, angry, discounted or I am wrong and I do not want to admit it.

Today *I* need to remember that discussion is the better path to follow. I need to hear and understand what the other person is saying, to try to see from the other's point of view. For too long I have argued, fought and produced enemies—today I wish to embrace the spiritual path of serenity and reconciliation. Also, I do not want to hurt anymore. Arguments hurt me. Arguments hurt others. I should push and scream but inside, afterwards, I hurt. My program today allows my ego to be balanced and restrained. I try to think before I speak. I consider before I react. However, when I do get into arguments and say hurtful and painful things that I do not mean, I am brave enough to say I am sorry.

May the God of peace, love and acceptance be seen in my relationships.

> *"A little theory makes sex more interesting, more comprehensive and less scary. Too much is a put-- down especially as you're likely to get it out of perspective and become a spectator of your own performance."*
>
> Dr. Alex Comfort

We make too much of sex because we are afraid of it. We abuse God's gift of sex by placing it out of context, removing it from the other things that make it meaningful, e.g., gentleness, trust, sensitivity, communication and commitment.

The performance becomes more important than the expression. The meaning gets lost in the event. God's precious gift of sex is abused by the sex act itself and it then begins to feed on itself. Compulsive sex is only demonstrated loneliness!

Spirituality teaches me to see all things as part of God's gift of wholeness and sex is an important part of this—but only a part.

> *God, in the awareness of my sexuality,*
> *may I discover a relationship with myself,*
> *others and You.*

"To teach is to learn."

Japanese Proverb

The more I learn the more I know that I do not understand. Life is full of new and wonderful information; paradoxes and confusion abound; every new idea leads to a further truth — and the journey seems endless.

In a sense we are all disciples; we are all learning from each other and the role of teacher and student is forever being exchanged. In my sobriety I am able to see how many wonderful things exist in the world — so many fascinating and interesting places to visit, so many loving and insightful people. God has given me so much, I am so grateful to be able to learn in God's garden.

Teacher, may I never stop learning and being a student in Your world.

138

"Liberty means responsibility. That is why most men dread it."

George Bernard Shaw

The fellowship of recovering addicts and their families rejoice in the freedom of life; the exchange of slavery to a drug or person for liberty; a life of choice, rather than meaningless compulsion.

But with the gift of liberty comes the weight of responsibility. Today I am responsible for my life. No longer can I say I do not know; no longer can I blame others for my disease; no longer can I manipulate in the playground of denial.

The spiritual program requires a maturity of lifestyle that involves responsibility — but the joys are immense.

Creator of liberty and responsibility, let me not forget to laugh.

"Tolerance is the positive and cordial effort to understand another's beliefs, practices and habits without necessarily sharing or accepting them."

Joshua Liebman

Today I am able to tolerate people, listen to what they are saying and if I do not agree with them, it is okay! I do not have to agree with people in order to tolerate or befriend them.

This is a new attitude for me and is part of my spiritual program. When I was drinking, I would not listen to people who had ideas different from mine. I would not tolerate people who had a different philosophy on life. Other religions were discounted as being cultish, crude or superstitious. I have learned that my disease of alcoholism made me very arrogant and narrow in my attitude to life — I rejected two--thirds of the world as being heretical!

Today I can tolerate and learn from people who view God, the world and morality differently from me. Spirituality is teaching me to be open and accepting.

God, may I find traces of Your love in different philosophies and religions.

"Faith has need of the whole truth."

Pierre Teilhard de Chardin

Faith is a journey that ends in God. Our understanding of imperfection teaches us to look beyond ourselves into the truth that is yet to be revealed. Our daily attitude adjustments bring us, step by step, to that truth and freedom that awaits us in the future.

Sufficient today to know that we are not God and nobody has all the answers. The hardest part of being a human being is accepting the limitations of our lives. Things happen without our involvement. We need not be there for existence to happen; there is life beyond me! God holds the world together, not me. Truth is in me but also beyond me. In this sense my faith is enriched by others, and at some point in the future we will all become ONE in truth.

As I look to the future I see the
Oneness of tomorrow.

"Money is the symbol of duty. It is the sacrament of having done for mankind that which mankind wanted."

Samuel Butler

S t. Paul said, "The laborer is worthy of his hire." In one sense money — how people pay us for the services we have performed — is symbolic of our value in the community. Of course, this is not always true and people can make money by dishonest and destructive methods.

However, in our society money is also a force behind much creativity and job satisfaction. The danger is to become a snob. Thinking that we are better than others because we earn more money.

Spirituality is about discovering the oneness of humankind and incorporating our creative difference — we can all learn from each other. Pretentiousness is indicative of insecurities that need to be dealt within our recovery program.

O God, let my gratitude be seen in my relationship with others.

"You have not converted a man because you have silenced him."

Viscount John Morley

I need to remember that I cannot force someone into faith. I cannot make someone believe. I cannot bribe a person into prayer. So much of my early religion was a "deal": you do this and you will get this. If you do this for God and the church, you will be happy and successful. There always seemed to be a payoff with God, or that was how it seemed.

I think many of the silent majority sense the same kind of thing: God has got lost in the business of religion. Spirituality accepts the pain, confusion and anger of this silent majority and says, "find a God of your understanding." Discover your power in your life — and then God will be perceived.

God, in my silence is the "shout" heard.

> *"Art flourishes where there is a sense of adventure."*
>
> *A. N. Whitehead*

Today I enjoy and am sustained by the adventure of life. The adventure of living. The adventure of living my life. For years I spent my time avoiding situations, avoiding people, avoiding me. Now in my daily recovery I need to participate and experience my spiritual energy. I want to meet new people. I want to travel. I want to work productively and earn money. I want to add something to this beautiful world.

I am discovering in my recovery that experiencing my creative spirituality makes me an artist. God is found in the hugs I give and the early morning hellos I shout to strangers. Today I am not afraid anymore. Today I am alive.

God, may I seek and find You in the small and mundane things of life; let me find You where I am.

"This could be such a beautiful world."

Rosalind Welcher

The beauty that I see in the world also reveals a sadness — a sadness in knowing that it could be a much more loving and accepting place for everybody. If only we would get together in our difference instead of demanding sameness.

We destroy so much God--given beauty by our desire to control, understand and arrogantly pursue a philosophy of selfishness—and we all lose.

But my spiritual hope for tomorrow comes in the creative choices I make today.

Let me be a good steward in Your world because it is Your gift to me.

*"Do what you can, with what you have,
where you are."*

Theodore Roosevelt

Because we are not perfect, we need only do our best. Because our recovery from addiction is an on--going process, we will discover that our best is improving on a daily basis. It is so easy to beat ourselves up emotionally by thinking that our best is not good enough. Even after years of recovery we still hear the old tapes: "People do not want to listen to you." "Is that all that you can do?"

We need to remember that the disease of addiction still lives in our recovery. However, our honest attempts at dealing with a problem or helping another with a problem — provided they are honest attempts — will usually be more than sufficient.

Today I accept my best attempts with gratitude and I am not too proud to seek the advice of another.

*God, accept the best that I can offer as an
instrument of Your peace.*

> *"My mother loved children — she would have*
> *given anything if I had been one."*
>
> *Groucho Marx*

For too many years I allowed myself to be treated as a child. I played the child role in order to avoid responsibility. Part of my people--pleasing was living as a thirty--year--old child! I was afraid to say no. Afraid to disappoint or hurt another's feelings. Afraid to tell my parents how they were hurting me by their need to control my life. God, when I think about it, I spent years feeling guilty and afraid.

Today I am willing to deal with this pain in my life; today I am willing to talk about it. My biggest relief comes in knowing that I am not alone. There are millions of us out there. The difference is I have a program today that enables me to talk about it.

God, help me to be child--like without being
childish. Help me to grow into maturity with a
smile.

*"The growth of the human mind is still high
adventure, in many ways the highest adventure
on earth."*

Norman Cousins

Today my life is an adventure. I am prepared for
the unusual; I expect the confusion of life; I revel in
God's reflected difference within creation: variety
and the acceptance of variety is part of my joy in
living.

I find God today in the "odd" things in life: dance,
relationships, Charlie Chaplin, jogging, my pet dog
and sincere hugs. The adventure we find in life
reflects our adventure in God.

Spirituality is seeing beyond the ordinary into the
extraordinary: "The Kingdom of God is within".

*May I always seek to find You in the smallest and
strangest of places.*

"That's one small step for a man, one giant leap for mankind."

Neil A. Armstrong

Human beings are able to do such wonderful things in this world. There is no end to what people can achieve when they behave responsibly and honestly, working with others to discover more about themselves and the universe. God has truly made humans in the divine image with all the power and creativity that that implies.

The danger that forever surrounds humankind is greed, pride and the misuse of power.

As a recovering alcoholic I understand this only too well. I wanted to be out in front, and ego made me arrogant and selfish. If this is true for me and other human beings, it is also true for governments, countries and alliances. Countries don't make wars, people do; countries don't have achievements, people do — and this universe must be seen as belonging to everyone or it will belong to no one!

Let us learn to enjoy and share Your garden and not destroy it.

*"Lord, grant that I may always desire more than
I can accomplish."*

Michelangelo

I must always "think big", not in an egotistical
sense but as an adventure in spirituality. When I had
a small God, I always remained a small person, with
small aspirations and dreams. Today I have an all--
embracing inclusive God that fills the universe.
Today I have hope in my dreams.

As an alcoholic I missed so much. I observed very
little about myself and God's world, people and
friends became inconsequential; nothing really
mattered except the desire to drink. My spiritual
potential was lost in my alcoholism.

Today I am realizing my potential and I can risk in
sobriety. My motto has become "go for it". Behind
my dreams is my growth. I have a sense of so much
joy in the world that I wish to enthusiastically
experience my life.

God, I am so grateful to be alive.

"He who begins by loving Christianity better than Truth will proceed by loving his sect or church better than Christianity, and end in loving himself better than all."

Samuel Taylor Coleridge

My program for recovery from addiction is spiritual and not religious. I believe that spirituality encompasses all that is good and noble in all the great religions of the world. It cannot be confined or limited to one religion or denomination. Spirituality stops the recovering person from looking for the differences; it stops the arrogance and prejudice; it stops the division and separations that feed the disease. Spirituality emphasizes the inherent unity of humankind. It teaches the most stubborn of people to hold hands.

God the Creator is revealed in the variety of the universe. I can find God in the sunset, the variety of animals, the love and care of family and friends, the excitement and vision of poetry and art, the inspiration of music. Spirituality is ...!

Kneeling before the beauty of Your creation I whisper "Amen".

"The fault, dear Brutus, is not in the stars, but in ourselves that we are underlings."

                          William Shakespeare

My addiction to alcohol led me away from "self": today in my sobriety I am beginning to understand me. For years I blamed others for my misfortunes but today I see that I was the enemy in my life. It was a cop--out to blame God, family, job or life for my alcoholism — I needed to take responsibility for myself.

Part of my recovery program today involves me not looking outside for answers but looking within. The answer is not in the stars, not in fate — but rather in the destiny I create by the decisions I make today. I, and I alone, forge my future.

O God, let me create a life that is pleasing in Your sight.

*"We need to make a world in which fewer children
are born, and in which we take better
care of them."*

Dr. George Wald

Spirituality is concerned for the physical. How
we plant seeds, do exercises and develop a healthy
food plan is as important as prayer, reading and
meditation. The body is part of the soul.

Also we have a responsibility for the future; for
those who follow us on this planet. The ecological
welfare of our world is spiritual. An irresponsibility
concerning childbirth reveals an arrogance that
does not belong to the spiritual program. The
satisfaction of our personal desires should never
hurt the lives of others — including the unborn.

*Teach me to have a spiritual responsibility to the
future.*

*"Show me a thoroughly satisfied man — and I
will show you a failure."*

Thomas Alva Edison

I need to strive for new things in my life. I need to push out into new areas and discover the richness of God's world. I need to explore the varied creativity of creation.

There is so much that I have not done because of the wasted years of my addiction. So much that I have not seen, countries that I have not visited, languages that I have not learned and experiences that I have missed. My compulsive and obsessive behavior left me a prisoner of self — and also a victim of self.

The spiritual recovery I enjoy today says it is okay for me to have things, enjoy things and do things.

*Help me to realize the energy and ambition You
have created within me.*

*"Old age is when you realize other people's faults
are no worse than your own."*

Edgar Shoaff

Age is a great leveler! I am on a journey to God and this involves many stages of experience — some good and some bad, some painful and some exceedingly joyful, some confusing and others understandable. These experiences will take me into a period of life called "old age".

Many people fear this period of life because it is connected with poor health, helplessness and death. I was afraid of age because a part of me feared the mystery of death. The uncertainty of death brought with it a lack of control! I am sure that guilt and fear of God were also involved.

Today I realize that we all have similar fears and concerns. Mystery brings with it a sense of awe! Today I have a loving God. Today God is involved in my life. Today, in my recovery, I have a perspective in my life — I am not all bad! Age is bringing balance.

*Thank You for the balance that comes with personal
forgiveness.*

"Everything one does enough of eventually generates its own interest and one then begins to believe in it."

Alan Dunn

I never thought that I could stay sober. For years I tried to abstain with no success. It was not the act of stopping that was different (I could stop three times in one week!). It was staying stopped.

Then somebody said, "Try stopping for twenty-four hours. If that proves too long, try stopping until the morning or for one hour or even for one minute … If the cravings gets too severe, call me but don't take that first drink!" My abstinence began in periods of twenty-four hours. Life is made up of days and we live in periods of twenty-four hours, so I live a day at a time. I was successful. I am successful. Today I have a number of years that are based on the simplicity of "don't drink today". I believe in it. I believe in me. And it gets better.

Creator of time, thank you for giving me the simplicity of days, hours and minutes.

"I like the dreams of the future better than the history of the past."

Thomas Jefferson

I am an optimist. I believe that things are getting better day by day. Today I believe that what happened yesterday need not happen today or tomorrow. Dreams can come true. I know this to be true. Today I have dreams. Today I have a hope for my life and on a daily basis it is coming true. My life is becoming more meaningful. Today my dreams have coincided with God's dream for me.

Now I love myself enough to speak out for me — and it feels good. Now my decision to embrace the spiritual life is not dependent upon others. Today I can dream to be me.

Help me to dream with my feet firmly on the ground.

"What is a man to profit if he shall gain the whole world and lose his own soul?"

Jesus (Matthew 16:26)

Spirituality brings with it a sense of priority in my life: first things first. Unless I discover me and have a love and respect for me, I have nothing to offer in this world. I am the center of my universe and through my life God is radiated. I am a part of God's creative plan and the pleasures of this world must be seen as secondary to my developing a right relationship with God.

My disease of obsession and compulsion wants me to place other things at the center of my life: food, alcohol, drugs, people, money, success, achievement and ego.

My spiritual program reminds me that my love of self is shown in my refusal of the first drink. If I am healthy, I can have the world; without me, I can have nothing!

Let me find Your Kingdom that is within.

"I do not feel obliged to believe that the same God who has endowed us with sense, reason and intellect has intended us to forego their use."

Galileo Galilei

An essential part of being human is the ability to think, reflect and reason. Spirituality is involved in our ideas and perceptions because that is historically how humankind has grown and been able to change. As Descarte said, "Cogito ergo sum — I think therefore I am."

The tragedy is that few people experience the freedom to think and create because of the stifling addictions that are epidemic in our society: food, alcohol, drugs, religion, work, money and sex. We are so afraid of what others might think or say that we never fully experience our spiritual selves and everybody suffers. Yet the risks in life make people great.

Help me to challenge what I do not believe in order to discover what I do believe.

"As long as men are free to ask what they must — free to say what they think — free to think what they will — freedom can never be lost and science can never regress."

J. Robert Oppenheimer

We need to press on in this wonderful journey of life because new discoveries await us in our tomorrows. Spirituality always brings joy in the journey. In the traveling is the fun for we will never reach our destination in this life.

The freedom to question is the discipline of science, and science is involved in the treatment and recovery of addiction. We must always be looking for better ways of treatment, more vivid ways of teaching and creative aids to recovery.

Science, and every other creative discipline, should be used in the treatment of addictions: God is to be found in the many.

Creator, let us remember that You gave humankind a scalpel and a prayer book.

"One of the weakness of our age is our apparent inability to distinguish our needs from our greeds."

Don Robinson

I was a greedy drunk. A greedy man. Spoiled, selfish and demanding. I felt that the world owed me a living and if I did not get my way, I sulked, cried or tried to hurt people. And this greedy attitude to life only made me sad, dull and boring. Greed, in this sense, could not work because what I was craving would never satisfy me.

Then I learned how to let go. Instead of demanding, I learned how to wait. Instead of consuming large amounts of alcohol, I practiced abstinence. Instead of expecting life on my terms, I went with the natural flow of life. I became happy, joyous and free. A miracle? Yes. I accepted my needs and with the acceptance came the satisfaction.

God, only when I accept my hunger for You am I truly satisfied.

*"I respect faith but doubt is what gets you
an education."*

Wilson Mizner

It is okay to question things. It is okay to say that I do not agree. Today I have the freedom to doubt opinions and attitudes.

In my childhood I was never allowed to do this. I had to accept the Bible because the preacher said it was God's word. I had to accept that only Christians went to Heaven because Grandma said so! I had to believe that Jews and Blacks were inferior because family and friends said so — and to doubt them was to be different. I was dependent upon an attitude towards life that I was uncomfortable with. It brought me pain, anger, loneliness and guilt in later life.

Then I learned that growth comes to those who are prepared to doubt or disagree with an existing system. God is to be found in the questions. Spirituality is discovered in the shades of life.

*O God, part of Your glory and splendor is Your
unending mystery.*

"Every dogma has its day, but ideals are eternal."
Israel Zangwill

For too long I lived in a box of rules and dogma. Life had to have definable answers and everything needed to be structured. Then the answers didn't seem to work. Nobody seemed interested in the answers I was giving. The world had moved on!

I realized that life had to be lived, not simply talked about. Having the answers to questions that nobody was asking (including myself) seemed a waste of time. I was uncomfortable. I was living in the past.

Spirituality is reality. It is okay to benefit from a tradition and then move on. I was not disloyal or a traitor because I had changed my mind. God and truth live in a changing world and if we are to grow, our perception of ourselves and life must change. Today I can accept this.

Give me the willingness to change in my life.

"God cannot be solemn, or he would not have blessed man with the incalculable gift of laughter."

Sydney Harris

I think the way to understand God is to begin to understand people! Sometimes we forget that we bear the "image" of God — and this is not so much physical as emotional, our inner selves, the soul. So much of what I feel, what hurts me, what causes me distress and pain I believe also affects God. Also the gifts, the creative intelligence and spiritual sacrifice that has characterized so many people in history reflects something of God. Involved in this is laughter. I believe that laughter is derived from God and is part of the spiritual gift God has bequeathed to every one of us: we need only discover it."

Let go — and let God." Sometimes we need to get out of our own way so that we can begin to laugh.

You gave the gift of laughter to be used. May it be used in the precious art of healing.

"Everyone should try to find a spot to be alone."
Queen Juliana (Netherlands)

Greta Garbo was reported to have said, "I want to be alone." Life brings its pressures, but we all need to find a place where we can be alone.

Alone — not to think or do — simply to be. We need time to simply rest in our lives. A time in the day which we can call our own, to have a visit with the most important person we have in our lives — ourselves.

To rest in self is to experience spiritual "self--ish--ness" — the joy of self--love.

And how much we look forward to setting aside a time just for heart and mind to center on the pathway to listening to God.

I need to be alone. In my peace I can unite
with You.

"There is no meaning to life except the meaning man gives his life by the unfolding of his powers."

Eric Fromm

My life was powerless when I was drinking. The drug alcohol stopped me from reaching my full potential — I was depressed, tired, angry, lonely and confused. Incredible as it may sound, I was the enemy to my life. By drinking alcohol, I fed the disease and made my life unmanageable.

Then I had a "moment" when I saw what I was doing to my life. The pain caused by drinking outweighed any advantages. I had hit my bottom. I began to change my life by refusing the first drink, and I began to experience a new vitality and potential. A new and creative life dawned. Friendships and relationships were possible again. God became understandable in the world. My power as a human being was unleashed in my sobriety.

God, may I discover my potential in the loving decisions I undertake.

*"We are citizens of the world; and the tragedy of
our time is that we do not know this."*

Woodrow Wilson

In recovery I have learned to "go home" to who I
am — and part of this involves understanding my
place in this vast universe. I am a child of God and
my "family" is not just my immediate blood
relatives, but also the millions of other people that
inhabit this planet.

God did not just make me. God does not just love
me. God is concerned for all people. As an
alcoholic I did not have this attitude and I was
always feeling lost and different. I became selfish
and narrow in my lifestyle. Other people were
tolerated.

Today I have a big God who has enabled me to
grow not only in my acceptance of self but also in
my acceptance of others. Today I am a citizen of the
world and it feels good.

*God, today I know what it is to belong to
the human family. And with this awareness
comes responsibility.*

"To be free is to have achieved your life."

Tennessee Williams

Y esterday's tapes: I need a drink. I can't exist without a fix. How will I get through the morning without taking something? Do people see me shake? Are people watching me? Where can I get money? The prison of addiction!

Today I am free because I took courage and asked for help. Today I am free because I still ask for help. Today I have learned to say "no" to the first drink and life is more comfortable and less painful.

Freedom is a precious spiritual gift that I work for on a daily basis. God is involved — but so am I. The freedom from alcoholism is only guaranteed by the creative choices I make and in the choice is the freedom.

God, my memory is the key to today's freedom; may I continue to remember.

"Nothing is so much to be feared as fear."
                                        Henry David Thoreau

Fear is a killer. It stops the God--given spirituality in our lives from taking shape and making life enjoyable. Fear is connected with doubt — doubt of self. Low self--esteem develops along with fear and in order for confidence to develop, the fear must be faced, confronted and talked about.

Fear is not going to go away because we wish it away or hope it away or even pray it away. Fear needs to be identified, located and seen for what it is — or, as in most cases, what it isn't. Fear of people, things, tomorrow or life itself grows as long as we forget that we are creatures of God. There is nothing that cannot be faced or overcome — as long as we remain drug--free. God is on our side — but we need also to be on our side. Fear is never stronger than our spirituality. We need to bring our fear into the light; then it can be overcome.

I ask to stay in the light of sobriety, not the darkness of alcoholism.

"Anyone who stops learning is old, whether at twenty or eighty. Anyone who keeps learning stays young. The greatest thing in life is to keep your mind young."

Henry Ford

My life is exciting today because I am learning and creating so much in recovery. Even things that I thought I understood have a new "ring". Words, ideas, relationships and the awareness of God are forever changing — usually for the better.

Sobriety is not boring. It is not stuffy, rigid or restrictive — and discussions (not arguments) within the fellowship of recovering people produces fresh insights. Today I am involved in the life of God. I am creating, healing and forever learning more about the mystery of love.

O Teacher of the Universe, let me seek beyond that which I understand.

"Only a person who can live with himself can enjoy the gift of leisure."

Henry Greber

As an addict I could not tolerate my own company for long. I was forever telephoning somebody, going over to a friend's house, inviting people in, creating an occasion so I did not have to think or, at least, think about myself. Being alone terrified me. I was terrified because I would begin to think about what was happening in my life and I did not want to face it.

Spirituality is reality. Some years ago I decided to encounter the real me, painful but necessary. I began to develop an awareness of who I am. Acceptance followed: I am an alcoholic.

Today I know me; today I like me; today I can love me — and this awareness brings with it a knowledge of God, self and my neighbor.

Today I can be alone without feeling lonely.

"Be still and know that I am God." In this "stillness" I begin to know myself.

"Less is more."

Mies van der Rohe

As a gambler, I always wanted more. I wanted to win more, get more, have more, spend more — always my energy was in getting "the more". But this constant and demanding lifestyle only gave me less. I could never stop to smell the roses. Activity robbed me of satisfaction. I was running through my life and missing it.

Then somebody told me to stop and rest awhile. Don't chase life; enjoy it. The gambling had become a compulsive and obsessive disease that was ruining my life. I was losing. I was not only losing money — but family, intimacy, life. I was so busy trying to win that I missed the pain and loneliness of my daily losses.

Today I choose not to do this. I accept that the "less" in my life is giving me more. I take responsibility for me, and I share freely with other recovering gamblers.

God, teach me to see Your power and beauty in what I can give up.

"A great many people think they are thinking when they are only rearranging their prejudices."

William James

An aspect of prejudice in my life is my refusal to listen. I tend to stay with my own thinking and I shut off people or ideas I do not want to hear. The problem with this attitude is that it does not lead to discussion, growth or change.

Spirituality is having the capacity to hear what others are saying, even people you may not like or respect, and also being prepared to live with and alongside confusion and difference. Truth is a many--sided diamond, and it cannot be comprehended from one viewpoint. I need to remove my prejudices if I am ever to move towards an understanding of God's truth.

I need to learn in my heart that there is the image of God in every person I meet.

Teach me to listen so that I may hear, so that I may grow.

"Write down the thoughts of the moment. Those
that come unsought are commonly the
most valuable."

Francis Bacon

My mind sometimes races with ideas: What should I do? What should I write? Where should I go? Phrases that could prove useful in an article. People I need to get in contact with, etc., etc. Many of these ideas come late at night and so today I have a note pad and a pencil at the side of my bed so that I can write down the thought and then go back to sleep.

I am not God. I know that if I say I will remember the thought tomorrow, it would be unrealistic. As an imperfect human being I take any help I can get. The pad at the side of the bed is invaluable!

Let me employ discipline as an aid to joyful and
creative living.

"The cruelest lies are often told in silence."

Robert Louis Stevenson

In treatment I said that I did not tell many lies — and although this was not true (hence a lie), it missed the fact that most of my lies were "lies of silence". It was what I did not say that produced the confusion; the pretended self--confidence that hid the pain and shame; the half--spoken truth that harbored the disease.

Communication is the key to any spiritual relationship and a sick silence creates the ultimate blasphemy. God created you and me to relate. In the interchange of our ideas is the miracle born. A sick, angry and ego--centered silence is our shouted NO to God.

O Creator of the paradox, let me see how the lie of silence can be used to destroy my world.

*"You'll never really know what I mean and I'll
never really know exactly what you mean."*

Mike Nichols

There is a certain loneliness in life with which we must all live; perhaps this is the price of individuality. I am not always sure that I know what I am feeling or thinking and so I know I cannot be absolutely sure of what you are feeling or thinking. Today when I say, "I know how you feel", it is with this reservation.

Another problem I face daily is finding words to express what I feel — language seems so inadequate. Words, although bridges to meaning, are often barriers to understanding. What I mean by what I say is often misunderstood.

This awareness provides me with the stimulus to be more precise, explicit and creative in my methods of communication and understanding. Today I consider more seriously what the other person is trying to say, rather than just listening to the words. Because I am sensitive to my difficulties in being understood, I am becoming patient with my neighbor.

Teach us never to become victims of our language.

"Do not take life too seriously. You will never get out of it alive."

Elbert Hubbard

When I used to take life too seriously, I was always miserable. I missed so much. I placed a disproportionate amount of energy on my own importance. I am not saying that I am not important, but I must learn to live within the structures of this imperfect world.

For so long I made myself the victim of this world. Every airplane I missed was seen as a personal abuse. I could not wait in a line without getting angry and developing a resentment towards everybody around. Everybody was expected to revolve around my world and I felt the world owed me a living! The result: unhappiness.

I needed to change or remain unhappy. Today I am learning to change and I am working on patience.

Thank You for the spiritual gift of balance in my life.

*"I have offended God and mankind because my
work didn't reach the quality it should have."*

Leonardo da Vinci

How I used to beat myself up! I was not good
enough. I was not attractive enough. I could not
speak properly. I was too small. My family was not
prestigious enough. I was boring. My breath
smelled, etc., etc. I never saw my value in life. I
could never see beyond my failings into my God--
given virtues. Sin was all too evident in my life!

Today I catch an egotism in my past criticism of self
and others! Who was I to think I should be perfect?
I could find fault with the Archangel Gabriel if he
came to be my neighbor. My compulsive disease
extended beyond drugs to negative attitudes about
life.

Today I see my value. Sobriety has restored my
dignity. Today I am in touch with that part of me
that is noble. Today in my sobriety I am a spiritual
somebody, not a nobody.

Let my desire for perfection be tempered by reality.

"Integrity has no need of rules."

Albert Camus

The benefit of a spiritual program is the development of integrity in my life. Integrity is having an honest respect for myself; it is respecting who I am and how I live in the world. Integrity also becomes a bridge by which I can reach my fellow humans. My respect for my life develops a respect for others. My determination to have integrity affects the way I treat you. Integrity gives me freedom to be — and this allows for an acceptance of you.

Of course I must follow some rules and guidelines in my life but today they are not written in cement. Today I can be flexible with me and this means that I can be flexible with you. My past need to control has developed into an accepting serenity that brings peace. My spiritual program forever teaches me to be free; now I can live.

I pray that I can see beyond the rules into the beauty of Integrity.

> *"In the republic of mediocrity, genius is dangerous."*
>
> Robert G. Ingersoll

Spirituality is a creative and positive energy that forever seeks new ways to improve and heal itself. Spirituality is never satisfied with mediocrity. God is alive in musicians, writers, singers and prophets — and always the standard of excellence is searched for; best can be made better!

As a drunk I often settled for convenience, no sweat, mediocrity. My motto was "Why bother? It can be done tomorrow." I had low energy. Addiction robs people of God's productive energy.

In recovery I seek the best because I believe I am the best; God made me — and I respect God's choice!

God, save me from the "comfortable way" that makes no demands on my genius.

"The devil can cite scripture for his purpose."

William Shakespeare

This quotation reminds me that the disease of alcoholism is "cunning, baffling and powerful". I am aware of the need to walk like I talk, to make the action fit the word, to live my program today rather than talk about it for tomorrow. Why? Because the disease can "talk program"! I have caught myself saying things that I do not practice in my life. I catch myself saying things to others that I do not live out in my own life. Today I am aware of my hypocrisy. Today I am aware of the disease in my life.

I need to be aware of this aspect of the disease because I am such a good talker, such a convincing talker, such a practiced manipulator! Today I know that I am not perfect, but that should never be an excuse to avoid dealing with my character defects. I must not con myself into staying sick!

I pray that I may strive to live the message.

"One of the disadvantages of wine is that it makes a man mistake words for thoughts."

                                        Samuel Johnson

Alcohol produced problems in my life. I was unable to control my drinking and the result was catastrophe. I hurt people. I endangered my health. I ruined my productivity. I became lonely. I felt isolated. I was forever getting into arguments. The police were often involved. People who loved me had to walk away from me for their own sanity. Alcohol made my life a mess!

Today I can see this and I am glad I made the spiritual decision to refuse the first drink. Today I am getting my life together. I am becoming a productive citizen. I have friends and relationships again. But I need to remember what I must never forget:

Alcohol + Me = Problems.

God, alcohol is a gift I can refuse.

"We should be careful to get out of an experience only the wisdom that is in it."

Mark Twain

I need to risk in life. I need to try again. I need to face life and not run from it. Early in my sobriety I was scared to try new things because I was afraid I might get hurt. I was afraid to express my feelings. I hid in the idea of simply not drinking.

Spirituality is about being willing to reach out into new areas, engage in new and different relationships, enjoy the richness of God's world. As I grow in sobriety I develop the capacity to react differently to painful situations and overcome them. I learn that mistakes can make for new conquests. That lasting joys and achievements are born in the risk.

Teach me to overcome yesterday's sorrows with today's optimism.

*"The one serious conviction that a man should
have is that nothing is to be taken seriously."*

Nicholas Murray Butler

For years I used to take myself too seriously. I thought that everything depended upon my thoughts, actions and decisions. Life was a series of agendas that had to be met; life was too serious to be joked about. I knew that I was not God, but I took responsibility for the whole universe. I had opinions on everything and everybody and I was, of course, always right.

As the years passed it grew painful being so responsible; my control produced stress, tension and loneliness. Then a friend said to me, "Let go and let God." I began to detach and laugh at my insane behavior. I laughed more as I began to accept my humanness. I discovered spirituality in the joke. God must have a sense of humor — after all, God made me!

*Help me to laugh at myself in my search for
the Kingdom.*

Let there be
spaces
in your
togetherness.

Kahlil Gibran

"Seek not to understand that you may believe, but believe that you understand."

St. Augustine

For years I tried to understand my behavior around alcohol and I only came away more confused. Sometimes my efforts to understand led me into dishonesty and manipulation. I drank because I was lonely, angry, happy, overworked or because I had problems with my parents. You see, I tried to understand "why"!

Science has no definitive answer as to why some people are alcoholic other than to postulate the disease factor, with the emphasized advice, "Don't pick up the first drink." So today I don't understand why I am an alcoholic. I also believe that I can never drink alcohol without having alcohol problems. This cherished belief keeps me sober and gives me a God I can understand; a life that I can love; and a world I can live in.

Oh yes — and I can remember where I have been today!

Help me to believe in what I know and to be content with the imperfection of my knowledge.

There is a paradox in pride: it makes some men
ridiculous, but prevents some men from
becoming so."

Charles Caleb Colton

Pride can be both negative and creative. I have experienced both in my alcoholic life. When I was drinking, my pride made me an arrogant fool, refusing to listen to the advice of others, always telling people what they should do, unrealistic in my demands on myself and others, lost in a fantasy of how I appeared to others. Pride became a mask behind which I hid my feelings.

In Recovery I am beginning to develop a love and respect for myself. I am proud of my achievements in recovery, and I am beginning to discover the "power" God has given to me. My spiritual program teaches me that I need to cooperate with God if things are going to happen in my life. God requires my involvement in order to work through my life. Today I am proud of my willingness to associate with the God of Truth.

God, let me always treat "pride" with respect,
mindful of its destructive attribute.

"Destiny is not a matter of chance, it is a matter of choice; it is not a thing to be achieved."

Willam Jennings Bryan

It is so important for us to see that we create our destiny. We create our futures in the choices we initiate today. During my addiction I was like a ship without a sail. I drifted through life and was tossed in a thousand directions. Today I am able to point myself in the direction I want to go.

Ido not believe that this attitude takes anything away from the power of God because God gave me freedom in the first place! God created me to be free and to have the gift of decision--making. God is not a dictator, and I am not a puppet on a string. God loves me enough to allow me to learn from my mistakes and to take personal pride in my achievements. Addiction made me powerless. Sobriety puts me in touch with my God--given power.

I am forever grateful and thankful for my involvement in my own life. I pray today that I might live responsibly a day at a time.

> *"Freedom is nothing else but a chance*
> *to be better."*
>
> *Albert Camus*

Human beings are not puppets. Sometimes when you hear people talk about God and prayer, they imply that we have no choice and that all actions in life are determined by God alone: a moment's reflection should make us hesitate from such a viewpoint. Murder, rape, child molestation and prejudice do not stem from God but are the results of God's gift of freedom to humankind.

Addicts and alcoholics need to comprehend on a daily basis that prayers that are not accompanied by actions are mere words. God's love for all people does not obliterate their need to love themselves through choice and decision. Sobriety and serenity should be experienced in our lives when divinity is revealed in our choice.

God, help me to appreciate my involvement in my
desire to be a winner.

*Without forgiveness life is governed by ... an
endless cycle of resentment and retaliation."*

Roberto Assagioli

So much of what I resent in others springs from
my unhappiness with self. I hate in others what I
know to be in myself: arrogance, pride, narrow-
mindedness, snobbery and dishonesty.

Today I am learning that as long as I refuse to
forgive others, I am not capable of forgiving myself.
Part of my denial is reflected in my attitudes
towards others. Those character traits I refuse to
forgive in others are buried within myself. I know
that without forgiveness there is no freedom — and
I wish to grow in freedom.

Today I am learning the difference between
forgiveness and acceptance. I can forgive other
people without accepting their lifestyle. I can
forgive myself and still see the need for change. In
my forgiveness is the hope for tomorrow.

*Creator, You taught that without forgiveness, there
can be no pure love. Help me grow in the forgiveness
of self and others.*

"The measure of man is what he does with power."

Pittacus

W ith my recovery has come a certain success, and with that success comes power. Power comes with the spiritual program, but it must be exercised responsibly. Just as the disease used alcohol to destroy my life, so it can use power to destroy me in sobriety. Power is a doubled--edged sword that has led many back to drinking. Certainly an abuse of power is not consistent with sobriety.

Today I am respectful of power because I know it can lead to an inflated ego or an arrogant personality that continues to destroy the quality of life. Today I surround myself with friends who will remind me of my roots.

Teach me not to use my White Anglo--Saxon Protestant heritage to belittle or patronize those from minority groups.

Teach me to exercise power responsibly.

191

"Doubt isn't the opposite of faith; it is an element of faith."

Paul Tillich

That part of me that does not know is vibrant in spirituality. Problems are part of what it is to be human and an element of doubt is essential. With the doubt comes the growth.

However, when I was younger, I was told that it was a sin to doubt; God demanded a steadfast faith and doubt could have no part of faith! I remember going to confession and feeling guilty and ashamed about my doubts — but I did doubt and doubt has always played a part in my life. In some ways I think that my religious doubts have been the most creative part of me — certainly they have enabled me to grow and build a bridge of understanding with others.

God, hear, through the doubts, my love of You.

"There is no must in art because it is free."

Vasily Kandinsky

Now I understand why the religious people of the past persecuted the artist. Now I understand why so many artists moved away from religion and grew beyond it. The artist is always searching for that which is different, that which cannot be contained or codified; that which is free: Spirituality.

As a drinking alcoholic I found it necessary to control my life; control my thoughts and behavior; control each and every situation — and it was depressingly exhausting. Today sobriety enables me to risk that which is new and different. Sobriety allows me to experiment and take risks in God's world. Sobriety is being free.

I am discovering more of me in what yesterday's artists wrote and produced. The musts of yesterday have been replaced by the shoulds and needs today. I am free to listen to and consider people because they are individuals, and not simply because of their credentials.

Supreme Artist, let me hear You in the whisperings of Your creatures.

"There is no sadder sight than a young pessimist."
Mark Twain

I meet so many young people who have aged because of their drug addiction. They have lost that spark of youth that is both creative and hopeful. They reveal in their eyes a powerlessness that keeps them prisoners of lethargy. They don't want to do anything. They mumble rather than speak. They walk with no purpose: young zombies! Addiction breeds pessimism.

Recovery is realizing that life need not be like this. True joy and happiness comes with the experience of self, rather than the confused experiences of chemicals. Reality is facing the pain and problems in order to rediscover the dynamic spirituality of a drug--free life. The "yes" to life begins with the "no" to drugs. Happiness and confidence are discovered in the "yes" to life.

Let me see beyond the gloom to the promised sunrise of tomorrow.

"Must the hunger become anger and anger become fury before anything will be done?"

John Steinbeck

I have a gratitude in my life today that stems from the daily recovery I enjoy in my life. Today I am happy, joyous and content; I am able to deal with the daily problems that we all have to face. I am grateful that I have a disease from which it is possible to recover.

However, there are millions of people who suffer in poverty or with diseases that cannot be arrested by a change in behavior or attitude: What can I do for these people?

Well, I can seek to pray for them daily. I can visit them or comfort their families when the opportunity arises. But more than this I can give money to the various research foundations that exist and require the support of the public. I have an awareness of my need to give. My feeling of gratitude must be earthed in the support of practical charities.

God, let the gratitude I feel enable me to give.

*"The foolish and the dead never change
their opinion."*

James Russell Lowell

P art of my understanding of spirituality is that I
will change. I will change my mind, my attitude and
my opinion. My understanding of sobriety is that I
will grow, grow in an understanding of myself, grow
in an understanding of God's will for me, and grow
in an understanding of other people. Today I am
not afraid to change my thinking about life.

During my years as an addict I was fixed and rigid
about everything. I saw it as weakness to change my
mind and opinions. Now I understand that I was
afraid of change, afraid not to have an answer,
afraid not to be seen as being in charge.

In treatment I learned how to understand
spirituality as reality; seeing things as they are, rather
than how I wanted them to be. I began to accept
that life is about change and that truth is a process
that we evolve towards.

*In my journey towards You may I have the
willingness to change.*

"Violence is counter--productive and produces changes of a sort you don't want. It is a very dangerous instrument and can destroy those who wield it."

John Gardner

I believed I wasn't violent when I drank but that is not true; I wasn't physically violent but I used emotional and mental violence. I did not hit, fight or mutilate people with my hands, but I could tear a person apart with my tongue. My sarcasm and criticism made people cry, feel demoralized and useless. Violence always removes the dignity from people — and I did this with my mouth!

Today I try to practice tolerance and patience, I count to ten, and when I do lose my temper and hurt a person unfairly or unnecessarily, I apologize. In my sobriety the anger, hate and need to hurt is slowly going. I am progressively getting better a day at a time.

Teacher, let me offer the hand of peace, not the fist of violence.

"To behave with dignity is nothing less than to allow others freely to be themselves."

Sol Chaneles

I believe that ultimately I can only be responsible for me. It is impossible for me to live another person's life. It is disrespectful to assume the role of decision--maker for another adult human being. People must have the freedom to grow and be themselves. Dignity is affording people this freedom.

Today I can see how I continued to keep members of my family sick by taking on a responsibility that was not mine. I can see how I was not giving dignity to my family; I was unintentionally withholding dignity from those I loved. People, especially family members, must be given the freedom to express their hurts. They have a responsibility to deal with their pain — because it is theirs!

I pray that I may give to others the dignity I desire in my own life.

"The ability to accept responsibility is the measure of the man."

Roy L. Smith

I believe the greatest insight into my life is that I am responsible; my responsibility is an important and dignified gift from God. My responsibility reveals my involvement in God's creation, in my life and my recovery from alcoholism. Greatness is in the choices I make, and the choices come with God's gift of freedom. Human beings are more than puppets on a string or automated machines. We are creative creatures who carry the burden and joy of responsibility.

Along with the acceptance of my alcoholism I also accepted the responsibility to remain sober in my decisions and lifestyle: such is greatness.

Thank You for giving me the responsibility to co-- create with You.

"I know that the twelve notes in each octave and the varieties of rhythm offer me opportunities that all of human genius will never exhaust."

Igor Stravinsky

There is so much to be gained in life. Just when you think you have exhausted all possibilities, a new insight is perceived, permutations and variations appear in abundance. An example is sobriety. I thought it meant not drinking but today I see that it affects all areas of my life — how I walk, the hugs I freely give, my acceptance of others, my willingness to trust and risk, my optimism for a new day.

Also God is comprehensive for me today. God is alive in church, the Bible and tradition and also alive in literature, scripture, sexuality and music. Today I can hear beyond the symphony into the unfathomable message of God's love for all creation. And always I hear something different and new.

Thank You, God, for Your messengers who love through the art of music.

> *"One must not lose desires. They are mighty stimulating to creativeness, to love, and to long life."*
>
> *Alexander A. Bogomoletz*

Today I desire to live. I have discovered value in my life. I have experienced personal self--esteem. I am able to feel again, talk, trust and laugh again. Today I desire to live.

But I can remember when I felt lonely, isolated, angry, shutdown and hopeless. The desires I had were destructive, desiring isolation mingled with alcohol. Then the pain became too great and I experienced a vital "moment". I realized I needed to make a choice — was I to live or die? I chose to live!

This was the beginning of my spiritual journey into self from which I discovered God and this world. Creative and positive desires were re--born in my life, and I am able to live and love again.

O God, may I continue to desire those things that do not hurt me.

"My life has been nothing but a failure."

Claude Monet

I can identify with Claude Monet because for years I considered myself a complete failure. For years I wallowed on my pity--pot until it became too painful. Whatever the pay--off was in the previous years had dried up, and I was left with a rock bottom pain that forced me to consider the alternative: I needed to set about doing something to change things!

Astounding! Impossible! How could this ever be? I was forever to be a victim of alcoholism.

"Not so." I heard a voice of hope from a recovering alcoholic who had made the change. Slowly I took small steps towards recovery and self--esteem.

I am failure so long as I consider myself a failure. I am what I create in my life. God requires my cooperation to make miracles in my life. My decision to listen to those who had achieved sobriety provided the seeds for my recovery today. I wonder if Claude Monet was an alcoholic who never heard the words of hope?

God, the only real failure is not seeing You in our lives.

> *"It is well for a man to respect his own vocation,*
> *whatever it is, and to think himself bound to*
> *uphold it and to claim for it the respect*
> *it deserves."*
>
> *Charles Dickens*

Nobody else is quite like me. Nobody else can view the world, experience the world, feel the world in the way I can. I am the center of the universe. Other people can love — but it is not the same as my love. Other people can offer the hand of friendship — but it is not the same as the friendship that I can offer. Other people can utter a kind word — but the phrasing of my words belong to me. I am unique and I must remember that. Even my space in the world is special. Nobody can take up the place that I have on the earth; you cannot get into my space. We may both be looking at the same scene, but I see it from my place in the world. Today I respect my uniqueness.

Let me continue to discover something of Your
unique image in my life.

> *"We are none of us infallible — not even the*
> *youngest of us."*
>
> *W. H. Thompson*

When I was a young man I did not want to listen to older people because I felt that they did not understand me. With hindsight I see that I did not want to hear what they were saying about my lifestyle.

Today, now that I am a mature man with a few years of sobriety, I must avoid having the same attitude towards the young, not listening to them because I think they are too young or do not understand! I must not repeat, in reverse, yesterday's mistakes!

None of us are infallible. We are not God. We can learn from each other if we have the patience to listen. Sometimes we need to seek the meaning behind the words.

> *God , teach me to listen with the ear of*
> *understanding and patience.*

> *"When I look back on all these worries, I remember the story of the old man who said on his deathbed that he had had a lot of trouble in his life, most of which never happened."*
>
> *Winston Churchill*

I know I can worry myself into the grave. I can project an incident into a calamity. I can make mountains out of molehills.

I worried about what people meant by what they said; I always looked for a hidden criticism; I worried about what people did not say; I worried about what people were thinking or were going to do or were plotting. If I had nothing to worry about, then I worried because I felt I should have something to worry about! I created most of the worry in my life.

Today I have a program that helps me deal with this. Of course I still worry, but I have a checklist that keeps me sane and allows me to laugh at the insanity of my projections. Today the worry in my life is less destructive and negative.

Let me bring my worry to You in prayer. Then let me sleep!

"Not ignorance, but ignorance of ignorance is the death of knowledge."

Alfred North Whitehead

How little I understood when I was living as an alcoholic. How little I wanted to know. Ignorance was bliss in my addiction. And the real tragedy was that I was ignorant of the extent of my ignorance! I had no idea how serious my alcoholism was, how pervasive in all areas of my life it had developed, how destructive and negative I had become until I was made to "see" reality in treatment. Reluctantly I opened my eyes to see my ignorance and I knew I needed to change my attitude if I was to recover.

The enemy of the spiritual life is ignorance because it stops us from realizing that the strength and healing power of spirituality has been given by God — all we need do is discover it and appreciate it.

I pray that I and others will have the courage to confront the ignorance in my life.

"It is not death that a man should fear, but he should fear never beginning to live."

Marcus Aurelius

For years I did not live. I simply existed. What many people take for granted I did not have: friends, vacations, job satisfaction, gratitude, family, communication and love of self. An aspect of my disease, my denial, was that I thought I was happy without having any evidence for such a feeling. Indeed, my lifestyle indicated progressive isolation. That's illusion. A recovering alcoholic priest shared that early in recovery he saw a sunset and remarked, "How long has that been happening?" Like him, I missed so much!

Life is to be lived or endured. My spiritual recovery means that every day I reach out to life and grasp it, hold it, smell it — and smile.

God of life, let me live today. Let my high be the glory of the day.

"The only question with wealth is what you do with it."

John D. Rockefeller, Jr.

P rosperity, if it is truly to be appreciated, needs to be shared. Wealth only makes sense when it is put to use for the benefit of the many. To horde treasure is to miss the value of that treasure. Money makes the world go around but it can only produce joy and excitement when it is spent or put to work.

This is also true for those who have a wealth of ideas or talents — they need to be expressed, shared and valued by others to be of any real benefit. A writer needs to write, a musician needs to play, a painter demands a canvas — and the world needs to appreciate.

God is at work in this world and requires recognition.

Let me find You in the talents that You have shared with me.

*"This great misfortune — to be incapable
of solitude."*

Jean de la Bruyere

Today I am able to live with my loneliness. I know the difference between being alone and being lonely — and even in sobriety I experience loneliness. But today I can live with it.

When I was drinking, I had an overwhelming feeling of being lost and isolated; today it is tolerable. I can live with it. It is part of being imperfect. I am not God.

The reality of spirituality demands that I do not escape into a fantasy that denies my feelings of loneliness. It is part of my journey towards God. I will never appreciate perfect happiness until I rest in God. This I accept. In sobriety I have many days of happiness and moments of joy — but I am, at times, lonely — with feelings of being lost. Today I can accept this — and talk about it.

I accept that part of me will be forever lost until I rest in God.

"Experience has taught me this, that we undo ourselves by impatience. Misfortunes have their life and their limits, their sickness and their health."

Michel de Montaigne

Nothing lasts forever. At times I feel sad, angry, resentful and ashamed — but it passes. In my recovery I have learned to live in my day and accept the consequences of that day. I can only deal with life as I experience it. Tomorrow is a new day with new experiences. And some of the experiences are painful. Reality teaches me this. At times I wish I could go through life without pain or rejection but I know that is fantasy. Sobriety does not mean that everything will be perfect — only better!

Nothing is so bad that I need to drink or use over it. Today I know that alcohol increases my pain; it is never a solution. God, who has given me today, will also give me a tomorrow — and time eases the pain if I work my program. Misfortunes are not worth drinking over. Nothing lasts forever.

Thank You for the gift of a tomorrow.

"Adversity reveals genius, prosperity conceals it."

Horace

Today I believe that the only way to understand God, the world, my neighbor and myself is through some degree of suffering. Pain and suffering are humbling in the truest sense; they stop you from being arrogant, selfish and prideful.

I know this because I was a spoiled child. My family tried to give me everything. Whatever I wanted was given to me; my way or no way! This sick love robbed me of humility and separated me from humanity. It made me feel different, selfish and placed me on a pity--pot. Being spoiled stopped me experiencing the real world and stopped me from growing.

Today adversity is part of life and part of being human. Not to grow through adversity is to die. To have everything is to experience nothing. To feel in life — to have emotion — demands adversity and pain.

Teach me to be grateful for the suffering that leads to growth.

"Ideas shape the course of history."
                                John Maynard Keynes

I get so excited about my sobriety because it has given me ideas. Today I can think, ponder and create. God is such a big idea today — every thing is involved.

For years I had made God a prisoner of the Church or an idea in history, but in my sobriety I have discovered God in art, poetry, music and literature. God is found in friendship, advice, sharing and sexuality. God is forcibly experienced in nature, sunsets, animals and the sea.

God can be found through my failures. God is perceived in suffering, loneliness and resentments. The acknowledgment of my disease has brought me closer to God as I now understand God.

My idea of God is alive and it makes me want to live.

May my ideas and thoughts always reflect Your beauty.

"Whatever you may be sure of, be sure of this —
that you are dreadfully like other people."

James Russell Lowell

F or many years I saw the differences and not the similarities. I was always considering how I was unlike other alcoholics, rather than perceiving the striking similarities. I kept myself on the outside, not only in recovery from alcoholism but also in life.

Then I heard from another recovering alcoholic not only "my story" but also my feelings. I belonged. I was with people who knew my loneliness, isolation, confusion, guilt and despair. I had come home to live amongst my people.

Thank You for enabling me to see that I am a
member of the human family and a recovering
alcoholic.

"I determine who is a Jew."

Herman Goering

P laying God. How well I remember this attitude
in my drinking days when, because I had said it, it
must be so! Arrogance and pride kept me lonely and
isolated.

Today my spiritual program teaches me to play God
in a different way. It requires that I seek to discover
the values I associate with God and live them out in
my own life. Because I believe that God is loving
and accepting, I seek to reveal these qualities in my
daily associations. It makes no sense to worhip a
God of truth if I continue the life of the liar. Belief
must determine change.

As a recovering alcoholic I seek to play God in the
joy, acceptance and love I show to myself and other
people. However, I know (oh how I know!) that I
am not God!

*Let my statements always be open to the pure light of
change.*

214

"Hear the meaning within the word."

William Shakespeare

When I hear or see the word "sobriety", I am made to think of relationships: my relationship with God, others and, more importantly, myself. Sobriety means humor, hope and joy. It means a silence at the center of my being that wonders at it all. Sobriety means a sexuality that is both noble and free — that risks rejection and criticism. Sobriety argues against prejudice and bigotry. It builds a bridge to the different and reflects on the creative variety of man. It allows me a God of my understanding, but also respects tradition and the ancient philosophies of the world.

Sobriety evokes a feeling that is beyond words. It echoes the spiritual life.

Let me learn to pray beyond words. Let my relationship with You grow in silence.

"What makes resisting temptation difficult for many people is that they don't want to discourage it completely."

Franklin P. Jones

U sually I am tempted because I want to be. I allow myself to get too close to the object of my desire or I invite the problem into my life knowing that I will not resist it. Then I use my imperfection as an excuse! In this way I manipulate my spiritual program and become dishonest.

When I first got sober, I did not allow alcohol in my house; I did not go to bars; I did not spend time with heavy drinkers; I avoided airplanes or places that I would associate with alcohol. This disciplined approach to sobriety worked. If you don't invite the enemy in, you won't get beaten up. I need to continue to remember these simple rules and not get complacent in my sobriety.

Let me keep temptation out of my life by avoiding it.

"The way to greatness is the path of self--reliance, independence and steadfastness in times of trial and stress."

Herbert Hoover

Today I take responsibility for my life. Today I take responsibility for my disease. Today I take responsibility for my recovery. I know I am not perfect and I have many pains and problems yet to face, but I take hope in my daily conquests. Nothing is too great for me to overcome so long as I have confidence in myself. It is my "yes" or "no" that makes the difference. In the power of my choice rests my freedom.

God, I thank You for my daily trials that ensure my victories.

"Nobody ever died of laughter."

Max Beerbohm

I knew that I was growing in self--esteem and confidence when I was able to laugh, express the belly laugh that proclaims that I am glad to be alive.

So many religious people are too serious. They seem to think that God disapproves of laughter and yet it seems the most natural emotion in the world. Sobriety is a statement that the pain is being overcome and the hope that is experienced will necessarily release laughter.

Laughter also stops us from treating ourselves and the world too seriously. I remember a professor telling me, "God created the world for fun. Find the key to life and enjoy it." Spirituality is that key.

Sometimes, God, in the silence of my car, my joy is so great and my gratitude so overwhelming, I can do nothing but laugh. Thank You for the gift of laughter.

"Man — a being in search of meaning."

Plato

Today I am on my way. With my sobriety has come a desire to understand — understand life, understand me, understand my relationships and understand God. Meaning — what is true? What is noble? What is spiritual? These are important to me today.

I no longer wish to hurt, damage, ridicule, destroy, fight, lie or cheat in my life. I've had enough of being negative. I've had enough of being lost and isolated in my arrogance. I've had enough of standing on the outside of life, feeling resentful and afraid.

Sobriety, for me today, involves my search for meaning — knowing full well that my understanding will always be imperfect and I can never comprehend fully. The ultimate answer is in living with confusion. I am not God ... but I still intend to reach for the stars.

God, my cry for self-awareness is answered in the journey and not the destination.

*"Education is helping the child realize
his potentialities."*

Eric Fromm

When I was drinking, I behaved like a child. I behaved not just like a child but childish. I was so dependent upon my alcohol, so addicted, that I never realized my potential in life. I never realized the gift of life!

Today I have a spiritual program that offers me the world; it sets no limits on my horizons; it encourages me to discover my potential and live it. Today I am learning new languages, visiting different countries and enjoying alternative cultures, making new friendships and, most importantly, discovering the "bigness" of God in this world. The education I have gained in my sobriety seems unending and unstoppable. Each day produces a new opportunity and a different experience. Every day is a time to receive.

Teach me to journey through the words into the experience.

"Thought makes the whole dignity of man;
therefore endeavor to think well, that is the
only morality."

Blaise Pascal

I think that human beings are very imitative creatures; we imitate clothes, hair styles, mannerisms and lifestyles. Our minds will be influenced by what we listen to and what we read. And what we think is very important to sobriety.

Today I make an effort to examine my thinking and check it out with a sponsor or in a support group. I know that my dignity in sobriety is connected not only with what I do but also with my attitudes and thoughts — when my thinking begins to go crazy, I know I am in a dangerous place and I need to talk. God created me with the ability to think, therefore, I need to safeguard the information I put in my mind.

Let me learn to develop morality of mind.

"If the blind lead the blind, both shall fall
into the ditch."

Jesus (Matthew 15:14)

I need to understand before I can teach; I need to listen before I give advice; I need to associate myself with the winners to become a winner.

For years I sought advice and direction from those who did not understand. They tried to help but they did not understand. Today I understand that part of my denial and manipulation was choosing those who did not understand to help me. This way I could stay sick!

My spiritual journey involves seeking out those who have something that I want, and being willing to follow their directions. I surrender to live.

Teach me to develop the spiritual ego that is
teachable.

"There is no more evil thing in the world than race prejudice ... it justifies and holds together more baseness, cruelty and abomination than any other sort of error in the world."

H. G. Wells

Something about me fears racism because I know that I am at risk. If a group of people can be persecuted or ridiculed for being different from others, then why shouldn't it eventually happen to me? With racism the whole world is at risk.

Also racism is the opposite of spirituality. Spirituality always seeks to include, bring together and unite. The world that God has made is ONE. All people and races are a family that must learn to co--exist together if we are to be productive and creative. In the variety is the strength. With the unusual and peculiar comes divinity. God is to be found in the confusions of life.

Teacher, let me have the courage to expose the inadequacies in my life.

"Money often costs too much."

Ralph Waldo Emerson

Money can be a curse. It can destroy people. Money in itself has no value. It needs to be used or put to work. The problem is that many people think it can work miracles, i.e., make them happy, give them self--esteem, bring love into their lives, remove their loneliness, cure their insecurities and remove their alcohol or drug problems! The historical list of wealthy casualties indicates that this is not the case. We cannot buy ourselves out of a disease! In this sense, money costs too much.

Because I have a compulsive nature, I need to be aware of my desire for money and the responsible way I need to use it. Spirituality involves the use of money. I need to be positive in my attitude towards money but also creative about how to use it.

Ineed always to remember that true wealth is found in my discovery of the God within and not in the clothes I wear.

O God, let me make money serve me; may I never be foolish enough to serve it.

*"The man who has become a thinking being feels a
compulsion to give to every creature the same
reverence for life that he gives to his own."*

Albert Schweitzer

Today I accept people. Even the people with
whom I do not agree, I accept. My freedom is
dependent upon my attitude towards others. My
respect is rooted in the respect I give to others. God
is to be found in my neighbor!

Nowhere is this more true for me as a religious
person than in my attitude to people of other creeds
— and those who have none! The spiritual life that
unites me to God and the world requires not only
acceptance of difference, but my personal need for
it.

But more than this; even those who hurt, abuse and
destroy need to be accepted from within my
spiritual self — because something of their life
exists in mine. In this accepting love is the daily
healing of my disease.

*May my acceptance of the tyrant lead to the
forgiveness of the self.*

> *"Faith must trample underfoot all reason, sense
> and understanding."*
>
> *Martin Luther*

An obstacle to my understanding the spiritual life was my intellectualization; my head was forever getting in the way of my heart. It was much easier to me to think rather than to feel; my faith was smothered by logic. My manipulating and controlling mind was stopping me experiencing the adventure of faith.

The poet in me grew as I began to trust others. God became alive in my confusion. The answer was in not having to have the answers. Today spirituality involves all the varied confusions and paradoxes of life that I have discovered in me and in others — and it's okay.

Today the love I give and receive is beyond my wildest dreams, and I smile at the joy of my confusion.

May my head unite with my heart in the daily maze of life.

*"The race advances only by the extra achievements
of the individual. You are the individual."*

Charles Towne

The spiritual program that involves a love of self
has made me get in touch with my individuality.
Although we can identify with other people's
feelings and situations, we are also not exactly the
same. Our dreams and aspirations are different, our
gifts and achievements vary, our personal
individuality adds to the variety of life.

My difference needs to be nurtured alongside my
spiritual growth, especially since being a recovering
alcoholic I am tempted to "please" the crowd.
Today my personal inventory revolves around my
needs, hopes and dreams that are realistic.
Spirituality is reality.

In helping myself to the abundant richness that is
within me, I am contributing to society and the
world.

*Thank You for making the world with such creative
difference; may I continue to risk in this knowledge.*

*"The tragedy of life is what dies in man
while he lives."*

Albert Schweitzer

Addiction progressively takes away the vitality of life. It robs life of meaning. Addiction isolates; it kills by atrophy. People, places and things lose meaning; everything becomes a chore and God is lost. We say to compensate that we are having fun — we say this a lot and at times we believe it, but in the silence of the night we know it to be a lie.

We lie to others and to ourselves. Sometimes we believe the lie! At this point we begin to die unless we take courage and confront the lie in order to live.

Today I live because I confronted my lie. I have discovered the spiritual power that was buried deep beneath the progressive addiction. And I am finding it easier and less painful to live.

May I continue to breathe a daily "yes" in my life so that I might live.

"Humankind cannot bear very much reality."

T. S. Eliot

I wonder why we find it hard to face reality? I preferred to escape from my problems, avoid who I was, not deal with issues of God, relationships or loneliness — and live in a world of make believe. However, it did not work. The pain of being a fake and living a lie became too great so I asked for help.

Today I am on a journey towards reality and it is a spiritual journey. I know I will never be completely real. A part of me will always be diseased. I must live and treat my compulsive behavior on a daily basis — but my life is getting better, and I am slowly growing in an understanding of who I am and what I need.

God, let me be as real as I can be.

*"If error is corrected whenever it is recognized as
such, the path of error is the path of truth."*

Hans Reichenbach

I believe that in order to discover spirituality in
our lives, we need to confront the disease, that
destructive and negative side of our lives. We need
to make the disease work for us!

For too many years I tried to avoid and deny my
alcoholism. I wanted to recover by osmosis! I did
not want to get my hands dirty with the reality of my
suffering but rather I wanted a miracle that was
really magic. to make everything different than it
had been for years. I did not want to face my pain!
But it does not work that way. If I am to get well, I
need to confront my disease, smell my disease, hold
my disease, pull and tug at the disease in my life.
Why? Because it is mine. I need to be in touch with
my disease if I am ever going to make the necessary
changes. I need to make my disease work for me —
that is spirituality.

*Let me have the courage to pass through the pain in
order to experience the gain.*

"Property is the fruit of labor; property is desirable; it is a positive good."

Abraham Lincoln

God is to be found in the physical. God is to be found in my body, my sexuality, the mountains and streams — and also in houses and real-estate. The luxury of comfort and good living is not incompatible with the spiritual life — indeed, the use of our property can be an opportunity for gratitude and sharing.

I know many people who use their comfortable homes for opportunities to develop sincere friendships. Luxury homes can be used for retreats and spiritual seminars involving music, dance and silence. Property is part of God's landscape in the world. God's love, joy and hope for humankind can be experienced by our creative use of property.

Let me use my property creatively.

*"To believe in sensible ideas is easy, but to
implement them involves sacrifice."*

Dorothy Fosdick

What am I prepared to sacrifice for what I
want? I remember the time I said I would do
anything. Today I know that anything must be
translated into something. No person, job or thing
can be allowed to come between myself and
abstinence. This love of self will enable me to love
others. But I must remember to sacrifice my desire
to please others and place my needs as a priority in
my life.

Today I know that if I do not love myself enough to
make sacrifices, then I can be nothing.

*In gratitude I give up those things I know
will hurt me.*

> *"Nothing will ever be attempted if all possible objections must be first overcome."*
>
> *Samuel Johnson*

There was a time when I never attempted anything because I said it can't be done. I could never get sober. I could never stand up to my drunken friends. I could never face my buried secrets. I could never stop gambling. I could never change my eating habits or stop using cocaine.

Then I heard the confidence and hope that was reflected in people who were recovering from these same problems. I heard people talk about what it was like, what happened and what it is like now. They told me I didn't mean "can't", I meant "won't"! They told me to take a risk, think positive, try.

Today, yesterday's objections are mere memories.

Thank You for showing me the light at the end of the tunnel. May I continue to walk in the light.

"Man's ability is derived from God and does not have to be acquired."

James H. McReynolds

I awoke this morning and remembered that sobriety and serenity are gifts from God that are freely given. I need only discover them within my capacity to be honest. I need only seek them in my new attitudes. I need only discover them in the spiritual program from my life.

God is alive in my life, and God's acceptance of me is guaranteed.

May I continue to discover more of Your beauty in my life.

"When you see a snake, never mind where he came from."

W. G. Benham

So many alcoholics have died looking for "the problem" that made them drink. The spouse, family, neighborhood or unemployment was why they thought they got drunk. They died seeking a reason. Alcoholics Anonymous clearly states that alcohol is the problem for alcoholics.

Alcohol is the problem! A statement that is so simple yet so profound in its healing. Today thousands upon thousands are choosing not to die by not taking the first drink. To see the problem clearly and honestly is the beginning of wisdom. O.A., ACoA, N.A., G.A., Al--Non and others have used these simple principles with profound results. Do I see the snake?

Teach me to avoid those things that cause me pain and destruction.

235

"A man who thinks of himself as belonging to a particular national group in America has not yet become an American."

Woodrow Wilson

Today I know that I belong. I am not alone. I do not exist outside of the human race. I am an important part of this world.

Addiction makes us feel different, separated and isolated. It keeps us divided within ourselves, our family and relationships. So long as it can do this, it wins.

Now I know that I belong. I make up a part of the whole. Something of this universe is mine.

I am not an island unto myself. I am an essential part of the human race. I am at home in my world.

> *"We are looking in the wrong places*
> *for happiness."*
>
> Robert J. McCracken

I sought happiness in the bottle. Others looked for good feelings in drugs, food or other people. Today I know that nothing that is outside of me can make me acceptable — acceptance must come from within.

I need to discover that spiritual place where I can be acceptable to me. Self--esteem is an essential part of my recovery and that can only be realized by making the spiritual journey within.

Today I seek to discover me. I want to know me —
because You created me.

"The worst sin towards our fellow creatures in not to hate them, but to be indifferent to them. That's the essence of inhumanity."

George Bernard Shaw

For years I was indifferent to family and friends. And the tragedy was that because of my alcoholism I did not know it! For too long I was unaware of my disease and its multiple implications.

Today I am not indifferent. Spirituality teaches me that I am not a spectator but a participant. I am involved in my life and, ultimately, in the lives of others. Today I seek to practice the principles of sobriety in every area of my life. I not only seek to be sober on a daily basis, but I also seek to be honest, open and tolerant with other people.

The spiritual goal of sobriety and abstinence has placed me at the center of the universe and I know today that I make a difference to my fellow humans.

Remove from me all attitudes of indifference and apathy. Make me a worthy steward in Your vineyard.

"There is no sort of work that could ever be done well if you minded what fools say."

George Eliot

Part of the risk in my recovery is arousing the displeasure of others. I know that I cannot please all the people — and yet my disease tells me that I must! For years I missed life's opportunities because I listened to negative and frightened people. Today I choose to shout my "yes" to life, and I ignore the fools. The fools are rarely friends. Rather, they seek to keep me in the same prison as themselves. If they truly loved me, they would encourage me to be imaginative and creative.

Today I have a joyride "letting go and letting God" because God is a great risk--taker!

I pray that I may always listen to the advice of others, but never miss my power of decision.

"Why would we kill off a good watchdog just because he could not fly?"

Frank Mar

God has created this world with variety and we all have different gifts. Some people make music, others write stories and many are practical at home or in industry. We need to understand what gifts and skills we have and develop them.

It is both fruitless and negative to spend our time complaining that we are not like other people — or are without their talents. Such an attitude stops us from discovering our own creative talents. We are so busy comparing ourselves with others that we miss our own uniqueness.

Today I enjoy discovering more about me and the abundant gifts that God has freely given to me. What about you?

I pray that I may be truly grateful for what I have.

"Your temper is the only thing that doesn't get better with age."

Anonymous

I lost my temper when I was in the wrong and wanted to protect myself. My temper was closely associated with my ego and pride; I hated to admit I was in the wrong.

Today I know that I am not God. I make mistakes and apologize. I don't have to have an answer. It is okay to be imperfect and human. And you know what I am finding? I don't lose my temper so much!

I pray that I may express my anger and discomfort without having a selfish temper tantrum.

"Nobody in this world is more secure than a man in a penitentiary."

Harvey S. Firestone, Jr.

In one sense it is safe to live in a prison — but at what price? To live is to be free and have the responsibility of choice. Addiction removes this freedom of choice; addiction takes away our freedom.

In sobriety I am involved in the joys of risk. I experience the pleasure and pain that comes with the responsibility of choice. Today I know I am living — yesterday I had to read about it!

God, I thank You for the confusing gift of freedom.

*"I have never doubted that God created man for
great purposes ..."*

Preston Bradley

I am special today. I know that there is a purpose for my life and that it is essentially good and creative. I know that beauty is not just in things that I can see ... beauty is also in me. Today I affirm my great purpose in this world ... to be the best that I can be.

For too many years I gave my God--given power away; I gave it to alcohol, I gave it to people, I gave it to a belief system that did not make sense to me. Today I am discovering the power that God has given to me, and I feel good about myself. Today I reclaim my divinity.

*Creator of this wonderful universe, make me an
instrument of Your peace.*

*"A man never discloses his own character so
clearly as when he describes another's."*

Johann Paul Richter

I was always so perceptive when it came to
assessing the character faults of others. I could offer
the best therapy and treatment to others; the best
advice in the world. I was excellent at "pulling the
covers" on a con artist — but always I missed me! I
never really heard my insights. I never followed my
advice. I always minimized my character faults.

Usually what I saw in others was reflected in my
own personality. The things I loathed in others
existed in me. The anger and resentments came
from a denial of self.

In sobriety I hear the advice of others. I don't
always like it but I hear it. I give criticism and today I
am growing in my acceptance of criticism.

In relationships may I see clearly my own reflection.

"The university exists only to find and communicate the truth."

Robert Maynard Hutchins

Today in my recovery I know I am a student of Truth and will hopefully be so until the day that I die. No longer do I search for the cheap thrill or the quick fix — now I desire lasting truths.

Spirituality is about finding God in things that are true and honest, good and wholesome, creative and positive.

I battle daily with that sick side of me that is greedy, selfish and dishonest — I'm not perfect. Today I know that the sick and dishonest way of living does not work. My history teaches me that it does not work. I was never truly happy knowing that the gains came at the expense of others. Now I am a student in the university of life, and I enjoy learning something new about me every day. Today I am able to listen — listen to those who are wiser than I. I know that I do not have all the answers — and with this knowledge comes freedom.

God, who lives in and through Truth, continue to radiate and illuminate my life.

"If other people are going to talk, conversation becomes impossible."

James McNeill Whistler

Part of my addiction was never listening to what people were saying. This was part arrogance, part denial, part fear, part control, part ego — the bottom line was that I did not listen. I was bored and unhappy with my life because I was a prisoner of my own thoughts.

My spiritual awakening — which I consider a process rather than an event, a process that is still going on in my life on a daily basis — was in allowing some new information into my life that led to admittance and acceptance. The day that I was able to admit that I was an alcoholic was the day I took a step towards acceptance.

Today I receive immense help and comfort from other people, especially recovering alcoholics. Two people experiencing an honest conversation are part of God's promised love for this world.

Let the words I hear be acceptable in Your sight.

"Style is the man himself."

Georges Louis Leclerc de Buffon

Style is involved in Spirituality, especially when it concerns the recovering addict. Sobriety and serenity are not just seen in what we say or do or in our ability to keep away from the first drink or pill; they are seen in our creative styles. How we feel about ourselves should be seen in the confidence of our gait and the concern for personal appearance. Personal hygiene is important because it reflects a love of self. Physical health and exercise reveal a desire and interest in life, fitness and energy.

Style may not make the person but it certainly reveals the individual!

May I seek to reveal the beauty You gave me with my appearance and style.

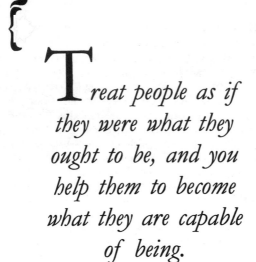

Treat people as if they were what they ought to be, and you help them to become what they are capable of being.

Goethe

"Optimism is a kind of heart stimulant — the digitalis of failure."

Elbert Hubbard

Today I am an optimist. I believe in life, and more importantly, I believe in me. I know that God cares and this brings me hope.

But when I was drinking I had a negative and destructive attitude in all areas of life; nothing pleased me, people were not to be trusted, everybody had a price, God seemed to be out for lunch, and life had lost its meaning. I was a sad man. I was a lonely man. I was an angry man.

When I was told to put down the drink and follow some new directions, I halfheartedly agreed. I met people who laughed, shared their pain and lived in the realistic now. I began to listen. Slowly I changed. Peace was within my grasp.

Today I wonder at my halfhearted risk that started it all — and thank God.

Teach me to look beyond the shadows to the sun's rays.

"Every man's memory is his private literature."

Aldous Huxley

What it was like. What happened. What it is like today. Memory. If I am to stay sober, I need to remember. I need to remember on a daily basis. I must never forget.

My life is reflected in my memory. The writing on the wall is really in my head, but am I prepared to see it and acknowledge it? For years I chose not to remember. I lived in a world of make--believe. People were exaggerating the facts! With denial at the center of my life I was able to forget the pain and drink again, only to awake to yesterday's pain again.

My memory is the key to my recovery. Spirituality is about seeing — seeing my life as it is, rather than how I imagined or hoped it would be. My pain belongs in my life because it is mine! Alcohol always works; but does it work for me or against me? My remembering helps me answer that question today and hopefully tomorrow.

Thank You, God, for allowing my yesterdays to forge my tomorrows.

"One of the greatest necessities in America is to discover creative solitude."

Carl Sandburg

I need to be alone. Being alone is not the same as being lonely. I need to be alone with me in order to love me, understand me, hear my needs and plan my day.

Also solitude is a spiritual experience because it enables me to center on what God is doing and creating in my life. Solitude enables me to think and cooperate with God's will for me in our world.

As an addict I was always running around being busy. Today I rest within myself in order to be more active and creative.

Let me be still so that I can enjoy my world.

> *"Humility is to make a right estimate of
> one's self."*
>
> *Charles Haddon Spurgeon*

To see yourself as a good person is part of the program of humility. To see your gifts and recognize your achievements is what it is to be a humble person. God does not make junk! Therefore, we should not act or behave towards ourselves in a way that would indicate anything other than that we are special.

All addicts and alcoholics need to accept this because for years we had felt guilty, lonely and ashamed. These attitudes helped to keep us sick.

Sobriety and serenity is recognizing our God--given uniqueness that makes us special. We can achieve great things as long as we continue to believe in ourselves.

*Thank You for loving me enough to become a
part of me.*

"All are but parts of one stupendous whole. Whose body nature is and God the soul."

Alexander Pope

I belong to this world, this mighty universe — but more importantly, it belongs to me. I have a responsibility in this world and to this world. No longer can I abrogate my responsibility. God created and is creating through me. What I say, what I do, how I feel is important. I am important. I am terrific — because God made me and works through me.

Sometimes I feel the one-–ness. I stand on a mountain top and look at the rolling hills beyond and I feel noble. The birds sing, the streams murmur and I feel a tremendous sense of joy.

But I also feel the pain of the world. The people suffering, the pointlessness of human violence and the injustice of prejudice. All this I feel, too.

Spirituality involves this mixture, the paradox of my being an angel in the dust!

Thank You for including me in Your design for life. I tremble at the responsibility You have shared with me.

"The only thing we have to fear is fear itself."
                              Franklin Delano Roosevelt

F ear is a killer. It is a killer because it drains us of life, energy and creativity. Fear petrifies the human spirit.

I spent a lot of yesterdays afraid. Afraid of people finding out. Afraid of the telephone. Afraid of where it would all end. Afraid of me! I did not realize that I was feeding the fear with my behavior. I drank myself into fear. The day I stopped drinking alcohol was the day I stopped giving energy to my fear.

Today I live my life without abnormal or unrealistic fears. Today I enjoy my life. I work through my problems. I am not afraid of my shadow. Today I love me.

God, may I always connect my unrealistic fears with
my behavior — and begin the change.

"Without work all life goes rotten."

Albert Camus

A spiritual discovery that I have made is that I work in order to be, not simply to exist. To work is human. Work opens the door to the meaning of life, and it stops life from being boring and dull. Work is creative. When I was drinking, I did not have this understanding of work and so it became a burden, something I had to get through, something I had to do for money or security. I missed the creative dynamic of work and how it could enable me to feel good about myself.

In recovery I work, create and grow not only in my job, but also in my leisure hours. Indeed the distinction between the two often overlaps because the program I take into the office is the same program I take into the party or disco. Today God is to be found in everything.

In the many aspects of my work I am made to feel alive.

"A liar needs a good memory."

Quintilian

I lied to impress. I lied to hide my guilt and shame. I lied to cover my mistakes. I lied to bridge the silence. I lied to fantasize. I lied to hurt and destroy. I lied to hide the real me. Then I lied to cover the lies. Then I lied to cover the lies I told to cover the original lies! So it went on. Endless. Exhausting. Meaningless. A part of me always loathed the lies I told. Then I grew to hate myself.

Today, because I understand spirituality to be based on truth, I try not to tell lies. When I do lie, I make an effort to correct myself and apologize. Today lying is painful for me. Today I try to use my mind, imagination and memory for better things.

O God, who gave humankind the miracle of language and communication, let me not abuse Your gift with destructive deceit.

"Science without religion is lame, religion without science is blind."

Albert Einstein

In the field of addiction we need to work together and listen to the professionalism we all bring: the answer will be in the many.

So often we divide ourselves up into ghettos of learning and miss what the others are saying — and the disease wins! This is reminiscent of the old days in the church when science was seen as the enemy, the world was flat and the earth was the center of the universe. Pride and ego kept people sick, isolated and afraid — and thousands suffered and died. However, people began to listen to each other and the world benefited from the shared wisdom.

As addictionologists and recovering people we need to listen to each other.

Help me to see You in the honest experience of every person.

"The good neighbor looks beyond the external accidents and discerns those inner qualities that make all men human and, therefore, brothers."

Martin Luther King, Jr.

As a drunk I said cruel things about other people. My prejudices hid my fears and insecurities. I condemned in others what I saw in myself. I deflected attention from me by name--calling others: sick manipulations. "Neighbor" was only a word that I could spell and interpret, useful for religious homilies or pretentious innuendoes but not something I really experienced.

Today I am able to be the good neighbor to many people, known and unknown. My recovery has brought people into my life. Relationships mean something; friends are important; the world is one. Black, Asian, Hispanic — all add a variety to my life that enable me to get in touch with buried feelings of my difference. In the stranger I discover something of myself; the foreigner has become both friend and neighbor.

God, I never cease to be amazed at the mystery and variety that is me.

*"To be able to be caught up in a world of thought
— that is being educated."*

Edith Hamilton

For years I didn't think I reacted. Things happened and I felt I had to respond — but rarely was it a considered response. I had no program for my life. I was like a boat without a sail.

Today I think before I speak. I talk things over with a sponsor or friends before I make an important decision. I listen to the opinions of others before I make a choice. Today I am caught up in a world of thought and it isn't simply my own. God knows my best thinking nearly killed me!

The world only makes sense because people share. It is the giving and receiving that makes life worthwhile. To be an island unto myself is isolation. I know what it was to be lonely. Today I desire a relationship of mind, body and feelings.

*Let me find You in my neighbor and be sustained by
the stranger.*

*"To love oneself is the beginning of a
life--long romance."*

Oscar Wilde

T oday I am able to say that I love myself. To
love myself is to love God and the world in which I
live. I cannot befriend, hug, help or create without
first having a relationship with myself. Without me,
there is no meaning to my life. I am the most
important thing in my life. This is not said to be
conceited but is an aspect of self--love. It reveals a
healthy pride and respect for my life. And it feels
good.

For years I thought that to love "self" was wrong
and sinful, a misuse of energy and time. What
people thought about me was so important; what
people said about me was a constant worry. And the
more I looked out of myself for meaning, the more
lost, isolated and confused I became. Then I heard
that God loved me and wanted me to love me.
Today I live and love through me.

O God who created me to love, let me begin with me.

"The greatest good of a minority of our generation may be the greatest good for the greatest number of people in the long run."

Oliver Wendell Holmes, Jr.

I belong to a minority. I am a recovering alcoholic. I use a spiritual program that keeps me sober a day at a time. I have a God that I can understand today. I do a daily inventory and make amends when appropriate, and I feel good about myself.

This spiritual program is reaching out to the world: gamblers, overeaters, cocaine addicts, the families of addicts, the children of compulsive people; obsessive people can all be helped by this daily program of acceptance.

Perhaps the recovering drunk has stumbled upon a miracle that can bring the world back to God!

God, the more I talk about my difference with people, the more they and I feel the same.

"Middle--age is when you begin to smile at things
that used to cause you to laugh."

Anonymous

T oday I feel so young at heart. I love to laugh, I mean really laugh; I love to play and act silly in my life; I love discovering my inner child that comes out to give balance to my life.

This was not always the case. Not too many yesterdays ago I was serious, depressed, affecting a smile that did not come from within. Alcoholism made me an unhappy man. Before I got sober my so called high had changed into a boring low!

I was middle--aged before I was thirty. Today I feel younger than I did twenty years ago — and it shows. You are what you drink. Today I am sober!

Thank You for the gift of play in my life.

*"We find it hard to believe that other people's
thoughts are as silly as our own, but they
probably are."*

James Harvey Robinson

Today I am able to laugh at myself. I even think
funny things. I sit at airports and look at the faces,
postures and mannerisms of the people passing by
and I smile, giggle and laugh in my handkerchief.
Then I think about what a funny man I am — so
ridiculously proud, so pompous about the silliest
things, so preoccupied about my own importance
— and it is funny.

Yes, today I am able to laugh at myself. I know that
people are funny because I know I am. At meetings
I hear people laughing about the day's insanities and
I can always identify. Even my relationships are
humorous. I try so hard to make a good impression
while at the same time offering the effect of
detachment — trying to be "cool".

God must have a sense of humor to have made you
and me!

*Thank You for the gift of humor — it allows true
humility to develop.*

263

"The worst vice of the fanatic is his sincerity."

Oscar Wilde

T he disease of alcoholism is "cunning, baffling and powerful", and it manipulates us to believe the lie. There is a point that we reach in our disease where we believe that crazy behavior is acceptable. Insanity becomes the order of the day. And when friends or therapists try to give us a message, we discount them.

How can we break down this wall of denial? Well, there is strength in numbers. If everybody we respect is disagreeing with us, then it is time that we change. If our isolation has become a source of martyrdom, then we need to reorganize our attitude for living. Insanity and isolation are often companions; they feed off each other.

We need always to stay close to our recovering community. Strength and sobriety is in numbers.

God, You gave me the message to become the message. Help me to live it in the recovering community.

"I cannot give you the formula for success, but I can give you the formula for failure, which is try to please everybody."

Herbert Bayard Swope

Part of my recovery is not that I never people--please, but that I know when I am doing it ... and I am doing it less!

My low self--esteem was revealed in the way I would say what I felt you wanted to hear, do what you wanted to do, go where you wanted to go — and for years I missed me. For years I missed my life because I was preoccupied with other people. And I wasn't honest. I hated being that way but I wouldn't admit it. Now I see that my guilt around my addiction led me into this sick cycle, and recovery is taking me out of it. Today I say "I don't want to go." "I don't agree with what you are saying." "I refuse to do that."

My dignity is being discovered in my straight--forwardness.

God, may I have the courage to share my true feelings.

*"A fanatic is one who can't change his mind and
won't change the subject."*

Winston Churchill

In my addiction I had a closed mind because I was
afraid to be seen to be wrong. I had to be right, I had
to be in control, and I had to be perfect. To say "I
don't know the answer" would make me weak,
vulnerable and human! So I developed a closed
mind: my way, my thoughts, my ideas, my life, my
God. And I was in pain.

Then I had a moment of clarity. I heard that I was
sick. I heard that if I really wanted help, I could
receive it. I put away the alcohol and I became
vulnerable. Slowly I faced the confusion of life and I
discovered the human race. I was no longer alone.

Today the spiritual life is more about living with the
questions than providing the answers.

I pray that I may continue to find Truth in variety.

*"Often the test of courage is not to die
but to live."*

Conte Vittorio Alfieri

There are many ways of committing suicide. The obvious way is to take your life — the ultimate escape. One can reach that point in life when there seems no hope, no purpose in living and death is attractive. Many alcoholics and addicts reach this point of despair.

However, there is a more subtle way of suicide, which is to kill yourself slowly by a sick behavior and a negative attitude. I was dying in a lifestyle that revolved around alcohol. All I wanted to do was drink — I didn't want to go anywhere, be with anyone or enjoy the thousand and one pleasures that life offers. I was dying in my life. I was becoming a walking zombie. I was committing suicide by degrees!

Today I can see this and I am glad I had the courage to live. My act of courage began with my "no" to alcohol.

Let me continue to live in my life.

"The mass of men lead lives of quiet desperation."
Henry David Thoreau

I thought that I was the only one who felt like I did. Nobody could possibly understand. I was different from everybody and needed to keep my life — my true life — a secret. I was living a life of quiet desperation! Then I went to a meeting for recovering alcoholics and heard somebody share my pain, my loneliness, my confusion, my addiction — my life.

I was lonely because I kept myself separate from people. I saw them as being different from myself, and so I remained the lonely and isolated victim. Strange how similar we are when we begin to share. When we get beneath culture, class and creed, we discover sensitive human beings trying to make sense of their lives. We need each other.

May I risk rejection in my spiritual need to share and be known.

*"I shall pass through this world but once. If,
therefore, there be any kindness I can show, or any
good thing I can do, let me do it now; let me not
defer it or neglect it, for I shall not pass
this way again."*

Etienne de Grellet

Today I know that God requires me to be
involved in my recovery and sobriety. God has
always wanted me to be sober but the miracle took
place when I wanted it, too. God's hands were
always extended towards me, the miracle happened
when I chose to embrace God. My sobriety
involves me.

Today I understand that sobriety is more than "not
picking up the first drink"; it involves quiet acts of
kindness to myself and others. God works through
me — through my hands, my smile, my voice, my
love and my acceptance. When an opportunity
arises for me to be ordinarily kind, I intend to give
it; God knows I have needed such kindnesses from
others in the past.

May I never avoid an opportunity for shared healing.

"If you're not allowed to laugh in heaven, I don't want to go there."

Martin Luther

When I was a practicing alcoholic, I imagined heaven to be a dull formal place, rather like a never-ending cathedral. Beautiful, but serious. My pain and guilt were so great that I rarely laughed, and when I did it was usually inappropriate and violent: I laughed at others!

Today heaven is associated with recovery. It is a place of joy, acceptance and forgiveness. A place where people can be themselves and where variety abounds. Christians play with people from other religions — and the atheists make the music! The laughter of peace abounds. I am at one with my Creator and all my brothers and sisters. I am home!

God of Love, when I hear the sound of laughter here on earth, I think what joy awaits me in heaven.

"Take away love and our earth is a tomb."

Robert Browning

Spirituality is essentially love. It is the love that suffers and grows in the acceptance of my compulsive and obsessive behavior. It is the love that requires a knowledge of self in order to give understanding and respect to others. Spirituality is that loving vulnerability that creates healing in recovery. It provides meaning to life and relationships.

The world is a creative place, and we will only find happiness when we begin to create. God has created us to take and make — give and receive. With the suffering, loneliness, struggle and acceptance comes a love that is real and alive.

Teach me to live in life and not merely exist.

"God is not a cosmic bellboy."

Harry Emerson Fosdick

My understanding of God is within the context of freedom. God is involved in this world, and allows it an autonomy. We are not puppets on a string. When things begin to go wrong, God does not interfere and make changes (usually) without our cooperation. The extent of God's love is revealed by allowing us a creative responsibility in our lives.

For years I did not understand this. I thought that if I prayed enough, God would answer all my prayers and come to my rescue. When that didn't happen, I grew confused, angry and resentful. What was I doing wrong? Where was God in my life? God didn't love me. Why wasn't God my cosmic co--dependent?

Today I love God's detachment. Today I grow in my freedom. Today I cooperate with God's miracle.

God, thank You for allowing me the freedom to fail.

*"Prayer is not asking. It is a language
of the soul."*

Mohandas Gandhi

At school I was told that prayer is "talking to God". Then I discovered that prayer is more than this — prayer is a relationship with God. It is a two--way system — I talk to God but I must also listen. Like any relationship that is going to work and grow, it needs time. I must spend time developing my relationship with God. I must create an awareness of this presence in my life because I believe God is always there for me.

But more than this, prayer is a yearning for truth within the center of my being. In prayer I get in touch with that part of me that will be forever restless until it finds rest, eternal rest, in God.

O God, prayer is my journey into You.

"You can't hold a man down without staying down with him."

Booker T. Washington

I know who was holding me down in my life. I was. I know who was bringing pain and sadness in my life. I was. I know who was making me the victim of addiction. I was. I would beat myself up and then complain about the bruises!

I did this because I could not see. I had not accepted or understood the implications of my alcoholism. Today I am beginning to take care of myself because I have accepted my disease. I do not choose today to be the enemy in my life — I have surrendered to live. I do not want to hurt anymore. I do not want to hide in guilt and fear anymore. I do not choose to be my victim today.

God, I thank You for the freedom to determine my life and my victories.

"Do not mistake activity for achievement."

Mabel Newcomber

Often I am running in circles and not getting anywhere. I spend forever doing things and yet I know I am not achieving anything. I am going nowhere in my life!

"Be still and know that I am God." I need to stop. I need to listen to the pain that is within. I need to relax in my gratitude. I need to rest in myself. Tomorrow has not yet come — today I take time for me.

God, I hear Your still small voice. Today I rest in me and discover Thee.

"Good people are good because they've come to wisdom through failure."

William Saroyan

Today I am able to learn from my mistakes because I can see that they really were mistakes! I was trying to play the game of life without a full deck. My big mistake in life was trying to drink alcohol like a non--alcoholic. I couldn't do it.

Drugs do not think; they react. They always work, and for me they worked against me. Most of my failures in life stemmed from a fundamental misconception — alcoholics cannot drink like non--alcoholics! This I now accept. And in a strange way that is difficult to explain, I am a stronger person for having lived through my alcoholism. God has become more real, the world is more comprehensible, my life is more understandable because of the pain.

If a part of goodness is knowing that you are not perfect, then on a daily basis I am becoming a good person.

God, who has created a world in which there is pain and failure, help me to accept both as vehicles to wisdom.

276

"It is human nature to think wisely and act foolishly."

Anatole France

I experienced blackouts in my drinking. Often I would wake up and not know where I had been, what I had said or what I had done. I would awake to peer through windows searching for my car. I would telephone to find out what time I had left the party and if anything had happened. Often as I bathed I would discover bruises or bleeding from an unremembered accident.

There were other times I knew what I had done, knew what I had said, remembered how I behaved — and yet still I went back for more. I drank alcoholically for years because my pride would not allow me to be alcoholic. I created the wisest excuses for staying sick!

Today my sobriety requires a wisdom that is based on reality.

God of action, teach me to place my feet alongside my best thinking.

*"Prayer of the modern American: 'Dear God, I
pray for patience. And I want it right now!'"*

Oren Arnold

How I appreciate those times when I
experience the gift of patience in my life, not as
often as I would like. That is an interesting point: I
am impatient about having patience!

Seriously, patience is when I recognize the need to
back off and allow God into the driver's seat,
resting in the knowledge that things happen in
God's time. This does not mean that I am not
involved, but it allows for God's comprehensive
plan for this world. I can experience patience
usually when I get in touch with gratitude. Once I
stop giving energy to the "I wants", the joy of
serenity breathes through my life and I can rest.
Sometimes I need to stop and say a loud and
resonant "thank you".

*God, let me breathe these words into my life: "Thy
will be done."*

> *"We are all here for a spell, get all the good laughs you can."*
>
> *Will Rogers*

When I first heard recovering alcoholics laughing, I thought I was in the wrong place. I was angry that they treated the disease so lightly. Then slowly I began to see that laughter is part of joy — a deep joy that comes from personal healing. Laughter is spiritual because it is a positive response to life. It is the noise of optimism.

And there is so much in life to laugh about — not only the funny things we did, but also the humor that abounds in living. How funny is our self-righteousness! How amusing we are in courtship. How ridiculous we appear when we pretend to be serious and in charge.

Laughter is the conversation of angels.

Let me see the miracle of humor in the gift of life — and let me be prepared to share it.

"The books that the world calls immoral are the books that show the world its own shame."

Oscar Wilde

In my addiction I avoided things that I did not like, did not want to consider. I hid from life and condemned things I did not wish to understand. My ego created a hypocritical purity that enabled me to judge, condemn and abuse the thoughts and idea of those I considered inferior to myself.

Today I try to live and let live. I do this not to avoid conflict or criticism but because I have found, through experience, how my ideas and attitudes have changed during my years of recovery. People who I would have condemned to Hell have now become my friends and mentors. Concepts and lifestyles that were once abhorrent to me are now appreciated and inspiring. What was once dismissed as immoral is today, for me a part of life.

God of Truth and Reality, help me to accept the difference that is in others.

"Freedom is not enough."

Lyndon B. Johnson

The gift of freedom requires the acknowledgment of the benefactor, God. To experience freedom without realizing its source is to miss the point; freedom requires responsibility.

When I was drinking, I demanded freedom without responsibility and I suffered. I created in freedom my own horror stories. I hurt others because I did not respect in them what I demanded for myself and slowly, ever so slowly, freedom slipped away.

Today I believe that my spiritual program reinforces my responsibility for my life. God has created me with free will and I need to respect this gift in others. If I do not respect others, I will never receive it. Dignity is a two--way street.

Thank You for the freedom to experience myself in my treatment of my neighbor.

*"I am not afraid of tomorrow, for I have seen
yesterday and I love today."*

William Allen White

Today I have confidence in my life and I am experiencing consistency in my behavior and attitude. In recovery things follow a natural progression and life is more like a series of curves than sharp peaks. As an addict, my life was forever going up and down, ecstasy followed by gloom; the "best ever" followed by depression; always black and white — no grays.

Today I have some balance and consistency. Things are connected and grow in the process of change. Sudden happenings and quick changes scare me because they are symptomatic of yesterday's disease and are not consistent with the spiritual life I seek. Today I have the peace of knowing that tomorrow will be something like today — and I am happy.

Thank You for the spiritual gift of consistency.

"The books I haven't written are better than the books other people have."

Cyril V. Connolly

Today I still have to grapple with pride, vanity and conceit. Today, thanks to God and my spiritual program, I am not so preoccupied with self, but the old tapes can still be heard: "Thank God I am not as stupid as that person." "I am blessed in not being like those people." "I suppose everybody in the room is looking at me."

Pride is still a big obstacle because it keeps me isolated from people. It emphasizes the difference between me and the world, rather than the commonality. Pride keeps me a prisoner of my ego and develops that cruel and sadistic streak in my nature that I know exists. Pride stops me being grateful because it keeps me too focused on what I am doing and I miss the beauty and splendor of my life. Pride keeps my nose pushed against the picture so I cannot see the portrait!

I can only change this proudful attitude by talking about it. The way for me to grow is to dump it ... today.

May I find me in the people I meet and share with.

"Forgiveness is the key to action and freedom."

Hannah Arendt

Early in sobriety I found it easy to forgive others but hard to forgive myself. This kept me sick and negative, even in recovery, because I was unable to practice self--love. I still blamed me and felt responsible for being alcoholic. I had not surrendered to the reality of alcoholism as a disease.

Then a moment of sanity was granted me whereby I understood that I was not responsible for being alcoholic, but that I am responsible for my recovery. And my recovery involves a love and respect of self. This knowledge brought a tremendous joy and freedom that led to action within the recovering community. Only by loving me will I be able to love you, and in both these ways I show my love of God.

May I always hold on to the spiritual power
of forgiveness.

"The first and great commandment is 'Don't let them scare you.'"

Elmer Davis

In my sobriety I still need to deal with fear. A fear of people, a fear of not being good enough, a fear of saying the wrong thing, a fear of not looking good enough — fear still haunts me in sobriety.

However, my recovery also tells me that I am a child of God. I am a beautiful and powerful human being because God not only made me, but I share something of God's precious divinity within me. I am good enough. In God, I can afford to risk. Love must begin with the recognition of self.

Today I must remember that people are not "out to get me". I need not make myself the victim. People are much the same inside, and we all need each other to survive.

Thank You for the power to live with my fear.

"Intelligence is proved not by ease of learning but by understanding what we learn."

Joseph Whitney

For years I learned things without understanding what the words, or the meaning behind the words, really meant. An example was alcoholism. Then a man said, "My name is Bill, and I am an alcoholic and a recovering human being!" Then it struck me; recovery from a drug — alcohol — was not simply about putting down the glass but about changing and developing a positive lifestyle as a human being.

The same is true with spirituality. It is not about being religious, going to church or accepting dogma. It is about finding God in my life, discovering God in the decisions and actions I take and seeing God in the world around me. Today I understand spirituality to be the link that unites all peoples and is centered on what is true and real.

May I continue to search for the meaning within the word and the harmony of communication.

"I believe the first test of a really great man is humility."

John Ruskin

An understanding of humility that makes sense to me is being aware of our limitations but still reaching for the stars.

For years I thought that humility was groveling in the dirt. Keeping quiet and acting obsequious. Being a religious doormat for others to walk upon.

Nothing could be further from the truth! Humility is about speaking your mind, fighting for your ideas and opinions, creating through effort, sweat and debate. When we are truly humble, our ego is based on reality — not fed on illusion. When we are wrong, we can admit it and be open to the ideas of others.

Humility is based upon a realistic self-love.

O God, let me humbly rejoice in Your gift of creativity.

"Art, if it is to be reckoned with as one of the great values of life, must teach men ... tolerance."

Somerset Maugham

There is something about art that is accepting, tolerant and reconcilable with difference. I have observed that artists — those who paint, write, dance, sculpt, design — are also people who are accepting and tolerant because they need the different in order to create and progress. Things cannot stay the same and art is the recorder of people's journey towards the truth; but humankind needs friction, argument, confrontation, rejection — yes, difference in order to grow and develop.

People say that artists are crazy, and I suppose this is true. But we need crazy people to take the world where it needs to go. In the crazy, the seed of genius is often buried.

God, before I reject the artist or the crazy, let me seriously consider the message.

"Art is not a thing; it is a way."

Elbert Hubbard

In the spiritual twelve--step program it talks about a God of your own understanding." This is a liberating concept that teaches us to risk and think "big". God is not only found in churches, temples and rituals — God can be found in the myriad of art forms. God is always to be found in the creative. Because art is always concerned with life and truth, God is always involved.

Today I am able to look for God in His or Her World.

In my recovery from the disease of addiction I need to discover the wonder and splendor of life that got damaged in my drinking days. Art can help me to feel again. It helps me to think and be concerned again. Art teaches me to be involved in life.

Thank You for the artist — another aspect of priesthood.

"I invent nothing. I rediscover."

Auguste Rodin

I believe that spirituality is given to every human being and we need only discover it in our lives to experience its power. The history of my life has been more of a cycle than a straight line leading into the distance. I am constantly returning to past events, reminiscences and experiences that were part of my yesterdays but converge into my present. I am rediscovering my yesterdays in my todays; the fruits of my tomorrows are planted within today.

So it seems that my journey is not simply forward. It also involves a rediscovery of yesterday in today. My life is a mystery that exists within God.

O God, with You eternity is ever present and occasionally I get a glimpse of it.

*"I am the inferior of any man whose rights I
trample underfoot."*

Horace Greeley

Now I can see my feelings of inferiority in the
assumed arrogance of my past behavior. Now I see
that behind the pride was the need to prove myself.
The manipulation was a cover for my insecurity.

At some point years ago I accepted the idea that I
was not good enough and needed to pretend to be
something different. The use of alcohol was part of
this disease process. Money, friends, fast cars and
debts were all drawn into the delusion.

Today I am learning to accept me. I am not a
millionaire, I will probably never be a millionaire
and so I do not need to adopt the lifestyle of a
millionaire! I work in an office. I drive a Ford. But
today I am happy. Today I can pay my bills. Today I
have friends who are involved in my life. Today I do
not have to put people down to feel important.
Today I have discovered that the people I treated
with disdain are just like me.

*I pray that I may receive healing and forgiveness
from those I considered inferior.*

"I am one individual on a small planet in a little solar system in one of the galaxies."

Roberto Assagioli

Spirituality develops a humility that is realistic. Realism teaches me that I am one among many. That does not mean that I am less than anybody else, but it certainly doesn't mean that I am above others.

Arrogance, fantasy and selfishness are characteristics of addiction that stop the development of true individuality. To pretend to be something we are not, or have a grandiose illusion about our own importance, misses the truth, misses our truth and misses our individuality.

Humility is treating people with the respect we would want, giving people the freedom we require in our life. Humility is perceiving our God--given talent and individuality.

I pray that I will remember that I am a part of, rather than the sum total of this universe.

"One man with courage is a majority."

Thomas Jefferson

Alcoholism made me afraid of my shadow. I became so petrified with fear that I could not enjoy my life. And I felt that I could do nothing. My disease told me I was helpless. I existed in an atmosphere of doom and gloom.

Then I experienced a "moment" of sanity when I saw that I was the problem in my life. My pain was being caused by my actions and attitudes. I took courage, confronted the disease in my life and I decided to take small steps towards recovery. I have built my confidence on that "moment" of courage I experienced years ago. I am not an island unto myself. I am not alone. God is with me in my life.

Teach me to have the courage to be what You have created. May I accept my miracle.

*"The great law of culture: let each become all that
he was created capable of being."*

Thomas Carlyle

We are capable of great things. This history of
humankind, although surrounded by wars and
unspeakable acts of violence, is also the history of
art, music, poetry and romance. Each person is
capable of great and noble acts — but do we want
to do them? We can be honest, loving and caring
people only if we choose to be that. The power of
freedom and choice is the determining factor in all
our lives. Each culture has imaginative and creative
features, but it is the people that make them
happen. Nothing will happen unless people decide
to make it happen.

So it is with the culture of recovery. The people who
make up the recovering community in all the
addictions are the people who make a decision and
act upon it. Talk is cheap and cruel unless it is
followed by an event. Decisions must be realistic.
We all have the capacity to be honest and kind.

*May I not only be grateful for my culture but may I
live to add something to it.*

You've got to be a fool to want to stop the march of time."

Pierre Renoir

My fear of the future gave me a fear of change. My need to control made me avoid any new or confusing ideas. My alcoholism wanted me to escape and hide in the past — tomorrow was too fearful to be contemplated. At other times — and this is why alcoholism is cunning, baffling and powerful — I would want to escape into tomorrow and avoid the reality of today.

Time and reality were to be "played with" rather than experienced. But time moves on, it progresses just like the disease, and if I am to be a winner in this world, I need to love with it. God is to be experienced in the march of time and today I want to be in a relationship with God.

Teach me to respect time as an opportunity for growth.

> *"Our concern is not how to worship in the catacombs but how to remain human in the skyscrapers."*
>
> *Brahanm Heschel*

Worship requires the discovery of true worth in my own life. True worship is not only historical and traditional but also contemporary. I need to discover not only the God of yesterday, but also the God of the modern city.

My past addiction to fantasy often made me place God in an unreal world. I was happy talking about the Jews, Romans and Philistines but I missed God in Las Vegas, on freeways and in local politics.

God is alive in this world, and it is tragic to make God a prisoner of history.

Let me find You in the place where I live.

"Tact is the art of making a point without making an enemy."

Howard W. Newton

An aspect of my recovery is not hurting people's feelings unnecessarily. I am learning how to say what I have to say without causing offense. Today I am learning to be tactful and respectful.

As a drunk I would say the first thing that came into my head without any regard for the feelings of others. I was often violent with words, sarcastic with comments and cruel in dialogue. Tact was a sign of weakness; gentleness and sensitivity were unmanly; my power was seen in forcing people to change their minds!

Today I do not wish to be like this. Today I desire to be tactful.

God, let me always express my opinion respectfully.

"The older I grow, the more I listen to people who don't say much."

Germain G. Glidden

I've noticed that an important part of my recovery is people--watching. I have fun watching people — at a party, on a train or in a park. I find the daily theater of life fascinating and stimulating. I also learn so much about me by observing others. I can identify with their mannerisms, actions and facial antics and intuitively sense what they are feeling. I see their fear, hesitancy and shame and connect it with mine. People are a mirror to my life.

Part of my recovery is developing that instinctive spirituality that grows through observation. People are forever communicating, sending energy and messages not only with words but by their existence — and especially by their silence. Sometimes a person's silence can be deafening! God is most alive to me in the lives and behavior of people, and part of my worship and prayer is observing the splendor and richness of my fellow human beings.

You, who have created the universe in such magnificent silence, touch me with Your stillness.

*"In matters of conscience, the law of the majority
has no place."*

Mohandas Gandhi

How I used to hate myself. So many times I caught myself pleasing the crowd, agreeing with people I did not understand or respect, laughing at jokes and opinions I loathed. How I used to hate myself!

Today I have a healthy respect for what the majority may feel but I also trust and follow my conscience. I know that to be in the minority is not necessarily to be in the wrong. My recovery insists that I listen to my conscience, the inner self that is based on a program of honesty, that spiritual cornerstone of my life that I have come to trust.

Now I can say to people, "I do not agree." Today I give myself permission to disagree with family, friends and colleagues.

*May I never follow the crowd because of the numbers:
God is one.*

"This land of ours cannot be a good place for any of us to live in unless we make it a good place for all of us to live in."

Richard Nixon

My sobriety has given me a comprehensive view of life and my neighbor. Today I believe that we are all connected and if I hurt or am hurt, then everybody at some level is affected. Because we are all children of God, it follows that we are all one big family — speaking different languages, having different customs, revealing different physical characteristics and complexions, requiring different satisfaction (both sexual and emotional), but we are still one big family under God.

This means I have a responsibility to all in the family and I can best exercise that responsibility by having a healthy respect for myself. I should treat people as I would want to be treated, allowing them the freedom and love I require in my life. I am the key to the world's needs.

God, let me find my neighbor in myself.

> *"A cynic is a man who knows the price of*
> *everything and value of nothing."*
>
> *Oscar Wilde*

I never knew the value of my life until I looked beyond it. For years I was so self--obsessed that I missed the joy and beauty of this wonderful world. I was so concerned with details and minutia of life that I missed the fun of living.

I now see that my behavior had its roots in my childhood. I was the child in a dysfunctional family. I became a parent to my parents. I took charge of everybody's life and I felt responsible and guilty. Everything was work and I did not learn how to play.

Today I am working on my recovery. I am dumping my feelings of guilt, shame and anger. I am beginning to understand that I am not responsible for my parents and I am beginning to feel free. Today I am learning how to play.

Creator of the dance, teach me the steps.

> *"A cynic is a man who, when he smells flowers, looks around for a coffin."*
>
> H. L. Mencken

There was a time when I always felt that life was out to get me. I always looked on the black side of life. I was forever being negative and pessimistic I would always be surrounded by sick and destructive human beings. Whenever people offered hope or tried to help me, I turned away and rejected them. For years I created the pain and misery in my life.

Then a close friend forced himself into my life and gave me a dose of "tough love". He made me see that I was wallowing in self--pity. He cared enough to intervene and tell me what I did not want to hear.

Today I have some years of recovery from alcoholism and I carry the message.

I pray that I may always love myself and others enough to take a risk.

"Better bend than break."

Scottish Proverb

Dis--ease: to   be   controlling,   stiff, uncomfortable and unbending.

Sobriety: being relaxed, comfortable and flexible in my personal life and my interaction with others.

Life: not a race but an experience; it is not an exercise but an adventure.

Before I accepted my alcoholism, I went through periods of dryness, when I was rigid, stiff and unbending. It was awful! Everything became a test, a job, a premeditated act behind a mask of cheerfulness. I was angry, resentful and in pain. My problem was that I stopped drinking to please other people, rather than accept the true nature of my disease. Dryness is controlled denial.

Today the sobriety I have gained from an acceptance of self has overflowed into an acceptance of life on life's terms — and I am happy.

Let the wind of experience continue to bend me in the knowledge of Your love.

303

"Kindness in words creates confidence. Kindness in thinking creates profoundness. Kindness in giving creates love."

Lao--tzu

It costs me nothing to say hello, and yet it might make all the difference to my neighbor. It costs me nothing to give a hug and yet that hug might make all the difference to a friend. It costs me nothing to listen to another's pain and yet the listening might make all the difference to another person.

Love is to be found in the small, ordinary acts of kindness as well as in the extravagant gesture. I need to seek God in the everyday happenings of life alongside the religious. Spirituality is in the smile that is real!

Today I know that I give only what I received — and I received a great deal. People loved me enough to be patient, they cared enough to telephone, they encouraged me with the gentle word of hope: I am in the flow.

God, You have created this wondrous patterned fabric of life — may I find You in its smallest detail.

"Justice is truth in action."

Benjamin Disraeli

It is not enough for me to believe that a thing is true, it is important for me to live out my beliefs. For too long I had a thousand beliefs that only kept me silent. A fear of displeasing others played a large part in my life of silence.

Today I understand justice to be part of what I mean by spirituality: I need to be seen to walk as I talk! I am uncomfortable when I remain silent in the face of injustice. As a recovering alcoholic, this uncomfortability is dangerous because it can so easily lead to low self--esteem, anger, resentments and relapse.

Today I know I can have a slip without taking a drink. I slip from where I want to be in my life. My personal integrity combines a justice that can be seen in my lifestyle.

O God of justice, teach me never again to hide in the lie of silence.

"The finest eloquence is that which get things done."

David Lloyd George

I know how to talk. I know how to sound good. I know how to convince a person of my good intentions — indeed that was part of my manipulation for years.

Today I try to walk the talk. I try to demonstrate what I say in the behavior I exhibit. The bottom line is action. Talking never stopped me from drinking — my physical refusal of the first drink was the start of my recovery.

God is to be discovered not merely in pious sentiments, as attractive as they may sound, but rather in the small steps of altered behavior.

Am I doing what I am saying? God give me the courage to live my words.

"I want to be the white man's brother not his brother--in--law."

Martin Luther King, jr.

Addiction is always about separation, ego, isolation and prejudice. The disease makes us feel different, less than, and we cover those feelings with false humility or we assume an arrogant and bombastic manner. Pride and feelings of inferiority put us on the defensive. It is not unusual for us to seek a scapegoat for our anger. Drinking alcoholics can be vindictive and prejudicial in their attitude towards minorities: Blacks, gays and Jews. It is a strange quirk of circumstance when a minority seeks to victimize another minority — because alcoholics are a minority group!

Sobriety is about a change in attitude and behavior. The spiritual acceptance of self must lead inevitably to the acceptance of others. The false pride and arrogance of our drinking days must give way to the vulnerable strength of sobriety. Now we are able to embrace our neighbor, regardless of color, class or creed.

God, teach me to seek You in my fellow humans and greet You in the stranger.

"Seeing is deceiving. It's eating that's believing."

James Thurber

It may seem strange to many but for years my belief system revolved around my eating. I believed that if I could eat I would be okay. Food for me was both the pleasure and escape I lived to eat. Feelings, good and bad, were surrounded and stuffed down with food. Some people drank to hide, used cocaine to escape — I ate to avoid the problems in my life.

Seeing was deceiving for me because I refused to accept the reality of my eating. I covered myself with clothes, avoided the beach, rarely looked at my body. I saw only what I wanted to see — and I was dying. Now I choose to face reality. This for me is the meaning of spirituality. I choose to show my love for me by loving my food, making choices around what I eat and eating slowly. Today I choose to talk about my problems, rather than eat them.

God, help me to accept my daily bread with gratitude and abstinence.

> *"Every saint has a past and every sinner*
> *a future."*
>
> *Oscar Wilde*

I must not allow the painful things of my past to affect what I can do today. Guilt is a killer if I allow it power in my life. I have made amends. I have apologized to those I hurt. Today I begin the rest of my life.

Alcoholism produces behavior that causes guilt and shame. In this sense it is different from so many other diseases. The shame and guilt I felt for years grew out of my alcoholic behavior and I need to remember that I am not responsible for being alcoholic. It is not my fault. However, with the knowledge and acceptance of the disease comes a determination to live responsibly. I have a sense of responsibility in my recovery. Spirituality involves being a responsible person. The awareness and acceptance of my past can help create a loving future.

Today I understand that in the failures of the past
are sown the seeds of greatness.

*"Appeasers believe that if you keep on throwing
steaks to tigers, the tiger will become
a vegetarian."*

Heywood Broun

Spirituality involves taking risks. But the risk has to be sensible, having the possibility of success. The risks I take today have a chance, usually a good chance, of succeeding and I always discuss "the risk" with a sponsor or recovering friend with some years of sobriety.

Today I take risks on things and situations that have the possibility of working for me, rather than against me. God has given me freedom and has taken a risk on how I exercise that freedom. God's love is revealed in the risk. But risk should have the possibility of success!

I pray that I will continue to take sensible risks.

"In solitude, be a multiple of thyself."

Tibullus

When I am alone and still, I get in touch with that side of me that is "the many". There are so many sides to me; the crazy and the sane, the extrovert and the introvert; the demanding and the submissive; the bigot and the compassionate; the religious and the skeptic; the happy and the sad; the comic and the tragedian; the child and the adult; the sick and the recovering.

Today in the silence of solitude I experience the many sides of me that I must live with — this is my spiritual reality.

May I always use my multiple experiences to relate to and understand others.

"Another good reducing exercise consists in placing both hands against the table edge and pushing back."

Robert Quillen

I am an alcoholic and today I choose not to drink. When alcohol is offered, I say no. I do not go into "wet places", spend time with drinkers or put myself in awkward situations. I assist my abstinence by the choices I make.

The recovering gambler avoids Las Vegas. The drug addict avoids sick relationships. The compulsive overeater must exercise the spiritual power of choice around food. "No" must involve both hands! For the recovering addict, talk must be accompanied by action. Some people, places and things must be avoided.

Spirituality is making my talk a visible reality.

"I hear and I forget. I see and I remember.
I do and I understand."

Chinese Proverb

I suppose the best way to learn a thing is to do it, practice it, demonstrate it, make it real in our lives. Spirituality needs to be experienced, not talked about. You cannot learn spirituality, get spirituality from a famous guru, read and acquire spirituality from a book — spirituality needs to be discovered in our lives. It needs to be found in body, sexuality, sweat, anger, morning exercise and kneeling in prayer and gratitude at the end of the day.

God, may You be real in my life.

"The spirit of liberty ... is the spirit which is not too sure it is always right."

Judge Learned Hand

I am free to make mistakes. It is okay for me to be wrong. I can say or do something that proves to be incorrect. I am not perfect.

Part of the liberty of being a human being is not being perfect; I am not God. In a sense this is a relief. I do not have to take responsibility for the lives of others or the crises in the world. It is okay not to have all the answers. Indeed, sometimes the spiritual life is discovered in not knowing and the answer will forever remain in the question. It is human to ask "why are we like we are?" But the answer rests in God.

God of Reason, let me be satisfied with discovering You in the questions.

"An atheist is a man who has no invisible means of support."

John Buchanan

The common cry of those who suffer from addiction is that they feel isolated. Not only isolated from self, family and friends but also from God. One reason for this feeling of isolation is teachings and attitudes that produced guilt, shame and fear. God was seen as a hammer with which society beat the addict.

Today, in an atmosphere of love and fellowship, we begin to look at these old attitudes and, hopefully, begin to change them. God can be seen in the hug as well as the sacrament; in the doubt as well as the dogma. In the honest sharing of fellow addicts, God is made known. God needs to be given a human face.

Teach me to grow in the virtues of tolerance and understanding.

"A good scare is worth more to a man than good advice."

Ed Howe

My fear of alcoholism helped me into treatment. My awareness of reality — "I am an alcoholic," — helped me towards recovery. I was scared into treatment!

I must never forget my frightening yesterdays because that can so easily lead to minimization and tomorrow's denial. I need to remember my pain if I am to continue to gain. My car accident, my abuse of self and others, my suicidal behavior should be feared, on a daily basis, because it is only one drink away!

God has given me a memory — I need to use it. My spiritual courage is in remembering my yesterdays so that I can continue to enjoy the sobriety of today.

May I see that a healthy fear comes from God; it is part of God's love for me.

"There is no place in active life on which thought is negligible."

T. S. Eliot

It is not a crime to think. It is not a sin to have a brain. To think is human.

However, so much of my past thinking was destructive and negative. The disease of addiction permeated every aspect of my life — particularly my thoughts. For years my best ideas justified my addiction.

Today I am open to a change of mind. I can choose to change my ideas. I am free to think differently.

God is alive in my willingness to change.

God, help my thinking to recover.

"Adversity is the trial of principle. Without it a man hardly knows whether he is honest or not."

Henry Fielding

The acceptance of my disease has brought me into recovery. If I had not known and confronted the disease of addiction in my life, I would not know the joys of sobriety and serenity. Spirituality involves facing my disease.

Today I believe that had I not seen my dishonesty, I could not fully appreciate honesty. If I had not recognized the lies and games in my life, I could never have appreciated the openness and freedom of sobriety. Owning my violence brought me to peace and tolerance. Facing my hell gave me a glimpse of paradise.

The disease was not only my prison but when accepted, became the key to recovery. Spirituality, finding God in our lives, requires a rigorous honesty that uses the past pain to experience today's gratitude.

God, it is through the acceptance of my failings that I can love the world.

"Faith is never identical with piety."

Karl Barth

Drugs make us artificial and unreal. They create a world of fantasy, rather than reality and teach us how to escape rather than live. Everything is exaggerated and dehumanized — especially the practice of our religion. Often for the addict, religion becomes part of the escape, a ritual that becomes exaggerated and theatrical, expecting magic rather than miracle.

Madonnas are kissed, promises are made, confessions become routine, prayers are mouthed and God is manipulated with the disease. Piety, the religious art of showmanship, keeps us a prisoner of the small god.

Faith takes seriously our pain and isolation and promises recovery only with change and accepted responsibility. We must walk our prayers and live our rosary!

O God, build Your temple in my heart and Your altar in my daily sacrifice of love to self and others.

"Peace without justice is tyranny."

William Allen White

Peace at any price! Not for me today. For years I sought a peace that was based upon the no--talk principle — remaining quiet, rather than causing upset or risking embarrassment. Such a peace was unjust. It only fed the disease and helped to keep me sick.

Today I seek a peace that involves discussing or confronting painful situations, often making me and others uncomfortable. Serenity is a peace that is arrived at after periods of pain — but a necessary pain.

In my life today I have the courage to speak out and make choices that are good for me; God is alive in my choice.

May I forever search for the peace that is real. May I find peace in the justice of my lifestyle.

> *"It is the test of a good religion if you can joke about it."*
>
> G. K. Chesterton

Today I am able to joke with God and about God. I am able to laugh at me swinging incense at a candlestick — and then swinging the incense at the Bishop! I smile at the determined seriousness of acolytes who receive communion while at the same time sticking chewing gum under the arm rail. I chuckle at the embarrassment of the baptism family when the baby pulls the plug out of the font and the holy water drains away.

Today I am able to laugh at God and the Church — it joyously reflects human imperfection, but at the same time reminds me of God's glory.

> *God, I contemplate You laughing at our pompous piety.*

*"Money doesn't always bring happiness. People
with ten million dollars are no happier than people
with nine million dollars."*

Hobart Brown

Today I understand that there is nothing intrinsically wrong with money. Wealth is not good or bad in itself — it is what we do with it. As a famous comedian once said, "I've been rich and I've been poor — and rich is better!"

But in what sense is rich better? I suppose in the freedom that it affords us, not only to travel and buy comfortable things but also in the way we can help and contribute to the lives and well--being of others. But to hoard money, be stingy with yourself and others, make a god of possessions or become compulsive about the making of money produces the same pain as any other addiction.

Money is to be used. It is usually one of the benefits of sobriety, part of what it means to say, "it gets better". Why? Because we are more responsible and creative as sober people and this brings its rewards.

*Help me to be a responsible steward of the
possessions You entrusted to me.*

"It is seldom that an American retires from business to enjoy his fortune in comfort ... He works because he has always worked, and knows no other way."

Thomas Nichols

For years I rushed around being busy — and I missed me. I spent years trying to please people by doing things — and I missed me. I was a workaholic, my value was seen only in what I could achieve — and I missed me.

Today I can relax in my sobriety; indeed sobriety has enabled me to relax. I can sit and do nothing and it is okay. Life is about "being" and not "doing". Spirituality is about taking time out for me because I am worth it. "Be still and know that I am God," said the psalmist. In the silence of self I have discovered the meaning of life and I have found God.

Thank You, God, for creating the feelings of peace that come from leisure.

"No man knows of what stuff he is made until prosperity and ease try him."

A. P. Gouthey

I must be careful that I do not get too comfortable and self--confident. I must be careful that I do not plateau at this stage of my journey into sobriety and relax in past achievements. Sometimes I hear the disease of addiction saying to me, "You've done all you need — now relax; take it easy."

Sometimes the sick voice says, "Listen to the stupidity of these newly recovering people: avoid them!" "You don't need meetings now — just sit and talk with your friends." Historically I know that when things are going well for me, that is when I need to be careful. A complacent and indulgent sobriety is dangerous. It leads to the disarming slip of arrogance and false pride.

I need to remember the pain of my yesterdays; I need to hear the newly recovering; I need to hear the pain if I am to continue to gain. My disease will forever speak, but will I listen?

Teach me to embrace a humility that enables me to enjoy a realistic sobriety.

"True friendship comes when silence between two people is comfortable."

Dave Tyson Gentry

P art of the spiritual life that awakens serenity is silence or stillness. "Be still and know that I am God." I believe that true friendship is divine. It is a special love that binds two hearts as one. It is a comfortableness that is the opposite of dis--ease. Friendship is necessary to recovery and it involves the sharing of feelings. Often the feelings are silent; unspoken emotions; cherished moments that exist in word--less--ness.

As a recovering alcoholic, I have a thousand friends who attest to the silent witness of love by simply being there.

Thank You for the joy of friendship that grows in silence.

*"Experience is not what happens to a man. It is
what a man does with what happens to him."*

Aldous Huxley

T oday I experience the joy of sobriety. Today I
experience God in my world. Today I experience
the peace and serenity that for years eluded me.

Experience is the key. It locates all that is in my life.
Experience allows me to appreciate what living is all
about.

Love is to be felt. Forgiveness is to be experienced.
Humility is to be lived in action. Hope is to be
recognized in the brightness of the eye.

Life is to be experienced. That is spirituality.

*May the God that I experience be reflected in
daily life.*

"All cruelty springs from weakness."

Seneca

My spiritual recovery means that I confront
my disease and remember sick attitudes and
behavior patterns. I would rather not talk about my
disease because it is embarrassing and shameful —
particularly my cruelty to people and animals. My
alcoholism made me lash out at the weak; yes, my
weakness inflicted pain and cruelty on others.

I remember this only to rejoice in today's strength
that allows vulnerability. My past weaknesses made
me act strong. Today my strength allows me to be
weak.

*God, the recognition of my past cruelties enables me
to forgive and understand others.*

> *"He that cannot forgive others breaks the bridge over which he must pass himself. For every man has need to be forgiven."*
>
> *Thomas Fuller*

My failings as an alcoholic help me to live with others today. The fact that I made and make mistakes helps me to have creative relationships today. Because I know what it is to fail, I can understand the failings of others. My weaknesses are a bridge to understanding my fellow human beings.

By contrast when I was drinking, I thought I was perfect, always right and this led to judgments, arguments and a self--imposed alienation.

Alcohol fed my arrogance and pride; sobriety helps develop humility and understanding.

God, I understand that even my failings can be made to work for me in sobriety.

"When I want to understand what is happening today or try to decide what will happen tomorrow, I look back."

Oliver Wendell Holmes, Jr.

T he writing is on the wall! My writing is on my wall and it is to be found in my life. My history of my life teaches me about my alcoholism. Alcoholism is a personal disease; it affects others through self.

Sometimes I am tempted to forget the past. Why live in yesterday? Because the events of my yesterdays affect my today. The future is forged from the recognition of my past. My disease grew strong in my denial. My recovery began with the acceptance of reality — my reality.

Today does not exist in a vacuum and my tomorrows are determined by the decisions I make today. I also know and believe that my recovering life demands a true recognition of my yesterdays.

Thank You for the historical progressiveness of my recovery.

"Self--trust is the essence of heroism."

Ralph Waldo Emerson

In my recovery I have become my hero. It sounds egotistical but it is part of my program of self--love. I have many other heroes but today I respect myself. Today I believe that God is involved in my life; an aspect of divinity exists within me. I trust me with my life, and I am proud of the daily choices I make for my sobriety.

Spirituality allows me to be my hero today because it is with my respect of self that I can truly respect others; the awareness of my dignity affords dignity to others; my personal healing brings healing to others.

Today I am the center of my universe.

Thank You for the awareness of the achievements and successes in my life; today I am my own winner.

Obesity is really widespread."

Joseph O. Kern II

To be fat is to be lost. It is a self--imposed isolation that keeps people sad. The fat is the result of an addiction to a series of chemicals in food that society finds acceptable; the disease of bulimia is widespread.

But it can be changed. People can and do get well from a compulsion around food by surrendering to the reality of their compulsion. The people--pleasing must be seen. The mask must be removed. The pain in the family must be talked about. Feelings that have been buried behind the food for years should be expressed. Feelings are to be felt!

We need not remain fat, and recovery begins when we begin to have hope; we begin to love ourselves; we begin to believe in ourselves.

O God, You hear the prayer of all Your children —
help me to hear my prayers, too!

"History is the seed bed of the future."

Leo Booth

I talk about my drinking history, remembering the incidents and losses, because I believe there is no gain without pain. To enjoy my sobriety I must share, on a daily basis, the reality of my disease. My pain is rooted in my history. I must live with my disease on a daily basis. I need to be aware of the disease process in my life.

This awareness requires a rigorously honest inventory of my past attitudes and behaviors; ignorance is bliss for the disease of addiction! The acceptance and awareness of my past is my treatment for today. The more I understand about my yesterdays the better my recovery will be today. My life has a history and my spiritual program demands that I understand it.

Teach me to face my past so that I can realistically live in my today.

"If we are not ashamed to think it, we should not be ashamed to say it."

Marcus Tullius Cicero

I was afraid to tell you what I was thinking. I was afraid to speak or be noticed. I sat for hours silent and at times I wished I could vanish into the furniture. I was afraid of my shadow.

This reveals not only my lack of confidence but my low self--esteem. I did not think I had anything to say, anything to offer, anything that might be considered interesting. I would laugh at stupid things to please people.

Today I speak out. I do not hide what I am thinking. I believe I have something to offer in the celebration of life. And it feels good. My spiritual growth is proportionate to my willingness to let you know who I am and what I think.

I celebrate my joy in living by sharing it.

*"I am an idealist. I don't know where I am going
but I'm on my way."*

Carl Sandburg

Today I am on the move. I feel an energy in my
life that gets excited each day. New people, new
places, new ideas all give me "a spiritual charge"
that help me enjoy my life.

I don't have all the answers and sometimes I am
confused — but today I can live with this and enjoy
it. God seems to be revealed more in the questions
than the answers; it is the problems that produce
the growth.

The journey of my life is an adventure that is free
and uncharted, even the pain and problems
produce a benefit that can be used for my recovery.
Nothing need be wasted.

I am the Way. I am the Truth. I am the Light.

"There is a destiny that makes us brothers, none goes his way alone. All that we send into the lives of others come back into our own."

Edwin Markham

I can remember when I felt so isolated and alone. I used to look at people talking with their friends, families playing in the park, lovers holding hands, and I felt so different and awkward. I always looked at life from the outside. I was the guy without an invitation to the party. The symptoms of addiction!

Today I know that my actions and behavior around alcohol reinforced these negative and destructive feelings. By my drinking I was perpetuating the painful disease in my life.

Sobriety led me into fellowship with others; it brought me into the family of recovering people. Today I am not alone. I have over a million brothers and sisters living a day at a time in a spiritual program. I have countless thousands finding joy, peace and serenity in sister programs. Today I belong in this world.

O God, thank You for giving me the need to give so that I might receive.

"Whenever science makes a discovery, the devil grabs it while the angels are debating the best way to use it."

Alan Valentine

Sometimes we can spend so long deciding what to do that we miss an opportunity. We can prevaricate to the point of impotence. Nowhere is this more true than in the science of relationships. We see somebody that we like and we go home thinking about what we could have said or done. We create happenings in our mind that never happened in fact. We miss the spiritual opportunity of risk.

For years I used to be like this. I always thought that I was not good enough, not important, less than other people: the syndrome of low self--esteem.

Today it is getting better. Part of my spiritual growth is reaching out to other people. Today I make a point of saying hello. Today I will ask for a telephone number, invite people to dinner, risk a relationship.

Let me not debate myself into sickness and isolation.

"The certainties of one age are the problems of the next."

R. H. Tawney

I was a religious bigot. I did not know that I was a bigot, but now I see how closed and narrow my thinking was. I craved for certainty because I felt it would give me security and happiness — but it never did. I argued dogmas that I did not believe; the plight of the unhappy hypocrite!

Today I live only in the certainty of the day. Today I know that what worked for me yesterday will work for me today if I am open to love, truth, honesty and change. Change is not necessarily difference if I see it as part of a process rather than an event. Yesterday is linked to today, and together they forge tomorrow. The one thing of which I can be certain is change. The God of Truth is revealed in the change; the acceptance of this fact is spirituality.

May I continue to grow in the spiritual life by my continued desire to change and be tolerant.

*"Men become civilized, not in proportion to their
willingness to believe, but in their readiness
to doubt."*

H. L. Mencken

A civilized nation is essentially a spiritual nation. A civilized person is one who seeks the truth and is willing to grow with change.

Sobriety is adventuresome because it is bigger than simply not drinking; it seeks to address all areas of life and all situations. An example is trust. When I was drinking, I trusted no one because I felt that everybody was like me — out for themselves! Today I know that the real enemy in my life is me; I am the one who brings pain into my life. I am beginning to love myself by my decision not to drink. I can trust today. I am beginning to trust myself and others.

*O God, who trusted humanity with freedom, help me
to freely trust.*

"I am the master of my fate; I am the captain of my soul."

William E. Henley

Things do not just happen, we make them happen. For years I thought that my getting well was dependent upon my family getting well. I rooted my recovery in the recovery of others. I was the typical co--dependent.

Then somebody said, "Why don't you start taking responsibility for your own life?" I thought about that remark for weeks. I spent nights dwelling on the implications of those words. I am sure that I had heard similar sentiments a hundred times but that night, that special night, I was ready to hear them. A spiritual moment.

Today I believe that such spiritual moments produce a spiritual process that I must keep alive. I am the deciding factor in what happens to me and what I can achieve. God has created me to be involved in my recovery.

May I always steer my life in the direction of truth and love.

*"Great minds discuss ideas, average minds discuss
wants, small minds discuss people."*

Laurence J. Peter

Gossip is ultimately a form of malicious
cowardice. It is a blasphemy because it seeks to
denigrate the human being that was made in God's
image.

As a practicing alcoholic I was a gossip. I
exaggerated and manipulated the truth with my
gossip. I made up stories against those people I had
a resentment towards; innocent people were abused
and victimized by my gossip.

Also I loved listening to gossip. The listener plays
an important role in the life of gossip because
without the listener it could not exist. It takes two to
gossip!

Today gossip is unacceptable behavior in my
program.

*Teach me to reach beyond my smallness into
Your greatness.*

> *"The certainties of one age are the problems of the next."*
>
> R. H. Tawney

Life is a process of change that inevitably produces problems; the fear of the new, the discomfort of old values being seen to be wrong, the confusion that so often accompanies growth. Problems are part of life and we can only escape them in death. (Even then nobody can be sure we will be free of problems!)

As an alcoholic I tried to run away from my problems by drinking. But the next day the old problems were still there and my drinking had usually brought new problems. Alcohol only produced a momentary escape but reality always returned.

Today, with the acceptance of my alcoholism and my decision not to pick up the first drink, I face my problems. I deal with my problems. I live with the problems of life.

Teach me to accept joyously the problems that life and growth inevitably bring.

> *"Wonder rather than doubt is the root of knowledge."*
>
> *Abraham Heschel*

Living with paradox is part of my sobriety. Things are never quite what they seem. When I think I have something figured out, I am made to be confused again — especially around my life, relationships, people, events and the universe. Life is both simple and incomprehensible. God seems to demand an agnostic faith! There is so much I do not know or understand.

But all of this leads to a creative and exciting sobriety. It makes life an adventure. It feeds that artistic part of me that is reborn in my sobriety. Things I used to dislike when I drank, I now enjoy. People and writers that once bored me now fascinate me; even modern art has a spiritual message!

O God, let the feelings of amazement always be a part of my faith.

*"Everyone is a prisoner of his own experiences.
No one can eliminate prejudices — just
recognize them."*

Edward R. Murrow

In recovery I am accepting that I am not perfect and some prejudices are part of my life — what it is to be human. On a daily basis I am trying to deal with them, and talking about them helps. They don't go away just because I talk about them, but I get them in perspective and I grow in an understanding of myself through the recognition of my prejudices.

Alcoholism made me into a fake. I appeared to be what I was not and my prejudices were part of the camouflage. My prejudices revealed my fears and my need to people--please. Slowly, in my daily spiritual program, I am discovering the courage to stand alone.

Teach me to love truth more than popularity.

*"Not every woman in old slippers can manage to
look like Cinderella."*

Don Marquis

Beauty is not what you wear or look like; beauty is within. We begin to love ourselves when we see the beauty that God has given to each and every one of us — forever. God's image and beauty is expressed through our attitudes and feelings, how we greet and listen to each other and the gentle dignity we afford to another human being.

For years I saw myself as ugly, boring, useless and stupid. This message came from parents who forever compared me with others — and for years I believed their message. I hid through my teen--age years and quietly tried to escape in food, alcohol and drugs.

Then after a crisis I met people who had felt the same but were now feeling different. They loved me until I could begin to love myself. Now I like me. Now I can love me. Today I can like and love you.

*Help me to see the beauty in the wrinkle; the power
in the pain.*

"There are two kinds of failures: those who thought and never did, and those who did and never thought."

Laurence J. Peter

In my life I know that I am guilty of both these failures. I remember making sand castles in the air without realizing that I could attempt to build one in my life. I would see somebody I wanted to talk with and imagine a conversation, rather than going over and risking possible rejection. Today I am able to risk — and I am now the possessor of a thousand memories that actually happened.

I am also aware of how thoughtless I was in my addiction. I would react rather than respond; create hostility as a wall to keep people out. Today I am able to think through a problem and apologize when I am wrong.

O God, You have made us to live in a world of happenings. Help us to accept the richness of life on its terms.

*"Man is a complex being: he makes deserts bloom
— and lakes die."*

Gil Stern

I am a mixture of good and bad. When I was drinking I could be cruel, sarcastic and violent and at other times loving, sensitive and thoughtful. Today in my recovery I know I can be honest, humble and creative, but I also carry within me a dark and destructive side that often hurts, lies and seeks negative power. What a mixture I was and what a mixture I still am! From all my many conversations with a variety of people I have discovered that this is what it is to be human.

Today I am able to accept this and develop my spiritual life. I am not perfect, but I try to improve my attitude and behavior. I am not God, but I can aspire to be the best that I can be.

Today I own the sickness in my life, but I also accept the responsibility for recovery.

With my feet in the dirt, I look to the stars.

*"All animals, except man, know that the ultimate
of life is to enjoy it."*

Samuel Butler

Today I choose to enjoy my life. Regardless of
the problems and difficulties that this day will bring,
I have an inner joy that comes with my recovery
from addiction. With a clear head and body — free
from drugs and chemicals — I can face today and
look forward to tomorrow. My life is to be enjoyed
not endured. My worst days today are better than
my best days as an addict. Spiritually I am free
because I have begun to discover me. God can now
be perceived in this world because I have sobriety.

*Creator of all play, I dance before You in my world
and I can stop to smell the roses.*

"Growing old isn't so bad when you consider the alternative."

Maurice Chevalier

What is the alternative? Not to change! To stay rooted in adolescence, youth, middle--age or whatever. Not to age is not to live, not to experience and not to grow spiritually.

An aspect of age, for which I am beginning to be grateful, is comparison; today I am able to look at the past and see the benefits of the present. Growth is measurable only through the tunnel of age. I suppose my fear of age is my basic fear of the unknown; fear of unmanageability and powerlessness.

These words remind me of the spiritual program that teaches me to confidently place my life in the loving arms of God. If I am responsible in life, I will be responsible in old age.

Teach me to use the spiritual perspective that comes with the gift of age.

"There is no higher religion than human service.
To work for the common good is the
greatest creed."

Albert Schweitzer

I enjoy doing things for other people. I enjoy seeing other people happy, seeing gratitude in their eyes and experiencing their hug of thankfulness.

Some people need to restrict how much they do for others and begin doing more for themselves — but I am happy and pleased with my service towards others. Why? Because I used to be a taker. For years I would walk away with all that you could give me and only thank you because I wanted to return for more!

In sobriety I am beginning to change this. Now I am giving and I am enjoying it.

God, the gift of service is a precious gift.

"The only courage that matters is the kind that gets you from one moment to the next."

Mignon McLaughlin

I do not have to have courage for a lifetime, just for the moment. I am helped by the philosophy that teaches me to live one day at a time, one hour at a time, one moment at a time. It is too awesome try to live my tomorrows today. Life is a process to be lived not a future to be anticipated.

For years I tried to anticipate what life had to throw at me, and I always came away confused, surprised and exhausted. I missed the joy of the moment by worrying about the future. What was my friend going to do? What happens if the police get involved? Will my mother telephone next week? Will my niece grow up to be alcoholic? Am I to blame? I had a thousand questions that I could not answer; nobody can answer for the future today.

I can only take responsibility for my life a day at a time. I developed the courage to face the moment and I became a winner.

May I avoid the temptation to seek the fantasy of tomorrow for the reality of today.

"At the back of every noble life are the principles that have fashioned it."

George Lorimer

God is to be found in the principles of life. The suggested patterns of behavior that lead to happiness, freedom and unity in the world. God is not just a good idea, an intellectual philosophy or other worldly entity — God is practical goodness that can be demonstrated and seen in the world. Principles lead to action; principles produce change in attitude and behavior; principles must have a practical result.

Sometimes you hear the phrase "walk the talk", implying that the principles we talk about should be evident in our daily lives. Also principles should be seen in the small things of life — being courteous, giving a smile to a stranger, offering a hug to a friend in pain. God is alive in the principles of life.

Help me to practice the principles I believe in.

"Man cannot remake himself without suffering.
For he is both the marble and the sculptor.

Alexis Carrel

I know that I have grown through my sufferings. I know that I am able to understand and forgive other people because I have been there, too. I know that I am patient and considerate because of my sufferings. My anguish keeps me "earthed". It stops me from playing God; it teaches me the reality of life — that life hurts! It is wonderful, joyous, loving and eventful, but it also hurts. For many years I hid my sufferings and pretended they were not there; the result was loneliness and hypocrisy.

God, may my sufferings keep me real.

"My God, my God, why hast thou forsaken me."
Jesus (Matthew 27:46)

In my sickness I was often angry at God. Angry that God did not do what I wanted when I wanted it done. I was a spoiled child. I refused to understand that suffering could be an important part of my spiritual growth. Today I know this to be true.

The biggest part of my suffering, then and today, is the feeling of isolation. Not knowing for certain that God hears me. Not understanding completely what God's will is for me. Not getting clear answers to my daily confusion.

The doubt is part of the faith. The "not knowing" is the answer.

God, may the daily doubts lead to a creative faith.

"The poor you always have with you."

Jesus (John 12:8)

Whoever said that life was going to be easy? A great number of people are placed in circumstances that are beyond their control and they die in helpless poverty. The poor are always with us. I cannot understand this dilemma and I have few answers for most of the world's suffering. However, I have a faith in God's love being realized beyond the grave for everyone.

But many of the poor are spiritually destitute by their own making. They choose to live lives that are consistently destructive and they refuse to change. Alcoholics and drug addicts are committing suicide by their lifestyle! I know because for years I was one. This produces a spiritual poverty that need not remain. This is a poverty that can be overcome. Recovery is finding the hidden treasure that is within.

Let me find Your treasure in the loving care I give myself.

"Liberty is the one thing you can't have unless you give it to others."

William Allen White

Spirituality is rooted in a respect for self that demands an equal respect for others. I can expect to be treated with dignity if I afford dignity to others. In the one is the key to the many.

For years I lived a compulsive life that only made me self--centered and spoiled, and it didn't work! I was unhappy, lonely and resentful. Today I find that the more I give to others the more I receive. Less is more.

In this sense it is much easier to be good than bad because goodness works!

Spirit of generosity, may I always reflect the gratitude that gives.

"Nothing in life is to be feared. It is only to be understood."

Marie Curie

God is on my side. Today I really believe and understand this truth, and it helps me cope with my fears. Now I am beginning to understand that I was the only real enemy in my life. With this new understanding of God I have the power of choice back in my life.

I do not have to stay in a sick process. I do not need sick and negative people in my life. I do not have to place myself in destructive relationships or in fearful situations. God is alive in my life and I am discovering the spiritual power of choice.

God, give me the courage to confront my fear and be willing to make changes in my life.

"You are free and that is why you are lost."

Franz Kafka

P art of my understanding of spirituality is that we have many choices and we live in moments of not knowing. Part of being human is that we have feelings of being lost. These feelings can lead to fear and loneliness or they can be seen as the essence of risk and adventure. With freedom comes daily uncertainties; nothing is predestined or made to happen — God is in the choice. Herein lies true greatness. The fact is that we do not have all the answers. We are not sure of the results. The joys are mingled with the pain and sorrows — such is the divinity of life. And yet still we choose to live!

Sobriety is accepting the reality of this uncertain life. My responsibility is accepting this freedom and making a daily choice not to drink.

May I accept my "lostness" until I return home to You.

357

"The People, though we think a great entity when we use the word, means nothing more than so many millions of individual men (and women)."

James Bryce

I am an individual. I am unique. I am special. Today I am able to enjoy my difference. I do not need to hide in alcohol, food or drugs. I do not have to put energy into being the same as friends or neighbors. I do not need to please people in order to feel good about myself. Today I am my own person.

God made us varied and different in so many ways, and yet so many of us spend our time trying to be the same. The effort exerted to achieve the lowest common denominator is exactly that: the lowest. My spiritual program demands that I be honest with who I am and what I feel. My self--worth is rooted in my individuality. In my difference is my soul.

May I always remain true to my individuality.

"Pessimist: One who, when he has the choice of two evils, chooses both."

Oscar Wilde

Today I am able to see how I was always looking on the gloomy side of life. The glass was always half empty! I can remember thinking that nothing good was ever going to happen, life was to be endured, everybody had a price and people were all selfishly out for themselves.

I projected onto others my own sickness, my own despair, my own pessimism. It was a suicidal existence. Today I choose to be a positive and creative person who refuses to be surrounded by negativism. My attitude in life makes all the difference to my enjoyment of life. Today my glass is more than half full and I am happy.

In the gift of choice, I recognize my potential joy.

*"Originality exists in every individual because each
of us differ from the others. We are all primary
numbers divisible only by ourselves."*

                                                    Jean Guitton

F or too many years I tried to be the same as
other people; matched their styles, repeated their
words, did what they wanted, lived to please a
crowd of people I did not really know — and they
certainly did not know me! I said other people's
prayers, quoted other people's opinions and
memorized the ideas of others — and I felt empty.

Today I value the lives of others but I am slowly
beginning to explore my place in this universe.
Today I accept the "specialness" that is me; that
uniqueness makes me God's miracle. Now others
are listening and benefiting from my life.

*O God, in my difference I am discovering
my service.*

"Great works are performed, not by strength,
but perseverance."

Samuel Johnson

Today I saw a large 200--pound man drunk in a parking lot. Last night I heard a frail mother celebrate ten years of sobriety. The difference? Perseverance. People get what they really want in life. If you want sobriety more than anything else, are prepared to go to any lengths, then nothing will stop you. Perseverance reveals the "walk" as well as the "talk".

Today I need to remember that what is worth having requires sacrifice and effort. God helps those who are prepared to help themselves. Today I intend to help myself to sobriety.

I pray that I may persevere through my fears
towards my goal.

"If thought corrupts language, language can also corrupt thought."

George Orwell

Sobriety for me means much more than not drinking or not using — it means the daily decision to be a positive and creative human being in all areas of my life: How I treat people. What I eat. The books I read — and how I speak! Not even my worst enemy would call me a prude but I think that bad language used on a regular basis is unacceptable in sobriety. Why? Because it hurts the listener and does not show respect for self or the God--given gift of communication.

If you have no respect for language, you will ultimately not grow as a spiritual person.

May Your words of love be reflected in my speech and writings.

*"I am a citizen, not of Athens or Greece, but
of the world."*

Socrates

My recovery has enabled me to see that I
belong; I belong not simply to a race or nation but
to the world. The freedom experienced in my
recovery enables me to embrace different cultures,
races and religions. Spirituality has brought
harmony into my life.

Today I can go where I please. I can learn languages
and communicate with people in foreign lands. I
can listen to ideas and philosophies that enrich God
as I understand God. The healing that I have
experienced in my recovery is more than
discovering my choice around alcohol, it is
discovering my choice around life. Today I am not
content to exist in my life, I choose to live it.
Welcome to my world!

*May I always choose to see and appreciate the
richness of my life.*

"And the Word was made flesh and dwelt amongst us."

John (1:14)

There is a beautiful fairy tale about a land where everybody had an abundance of "warm fuzzies" that they exchanged with each other and shared with each other. Everything in this land was wonderful because all the people were generously giving and receiving warm fuzzies.

Then a rumor began that there was to be a shortage of warm fuzzies, and people began to hoard and selfishly protect their supply of warm fuzzies. At this point, "cold pricklies" were introduced into the land. Sadness, pain, tension and persecution developed in the land, and the growth of the cold pricklies kept people separated, fearful and alone.

The tragedy of this tale is that the rumor was not true! As long as people generously share their warm fuzzies, they will never disappear. The warm fuzzies only disappear when they are not shared. The more we give, the more we receive. Abundance rests in giving, never hoarding!

Creator, may I always be generous with all that You have given me.

"The only thing necessary for the triumph of evil is for good men to do nothing."

Edmund Burke

I read about the Holocaust and I am ashamed. I am ashamed to belong to the human race that allowed, by an overwhelming silence, the slaughter of millions. The ultimate in people--pleasing is to do nothing. The fear of being an outcast or traitor allows the addiction to Power to develop. Power is an addiction that is rarely discussed in society. And yet evil needs people and politics to function — alone it is but a word.

With this new day I seek to be involved in the good life. Today I am not afraid to stand alone for what I believe to be the principles of a God--given spirituality. I know evil because I know myself. I know tyranny and injustice because for years I perpetrated negativity in my life. Now I choose to say no. Today I seek to make amends for past wrongs by being rigorously honest in all my affairs. Because I know what it is to hate, I seek to love. I wish to be responsible in God's world.

Teach me not only to learn from past mistakes but translate this knowledge into action.

"Sin has many tools, but a lie is the handle that fits them all."

Oliver Wendell Holmes

To lie is to rob life of meaning. In my addiction I was a liar, not just by what I said but by what I did, what I left unsaid and by my manipulation with half--truths. All lies shut out truth making us prisoners of fantasy and illusion. The world becomes what we want it to be rather than what it is — and reality is lost. Liars are forced into the prison of loneliness, despair and isolation because nobody can know them, nobody can understand them. Their language and communication are ego--centered. Liars are not living in the real world. They are living in their own world, with their own rules and definitions. The lies are the killing wounds, and they are self--inflicted.

Today I prefer the pain of truth to the passing satisfaction of the lie — and the habit of telling the truth is growing in me!

God of Truth, may You ever be reflected in the life I seek to live.

"Humor is an affirmation of dignity, a declaration of man's superiority to all that befalls him."

Romain Gary

Today I laugh at myself. Today I need to laugh at myself in order to stay sane. Today I choose not to take myself too seriously.

When I tell jokes about the alcoholic, I am not belittling the person. I am making fun of the disease that nearly killed me. For me to live with the disease, I need to be able to laugh at the disease — in this way I stop it from having power in my life.

Also I catch something of the symptoms of the disease in the jokes: the grandiosity, arrogance, manipulation, insanity, ego, selfishness and exaggeration. The joke allows me to face reality with a smile.

O God, thank You for the healing gift of humor.

"The madman who knows that he is mad is close to sanity."

Juan Ruiz de Alarcon

An alcoholic who continues to drink is committing suicide. An addict who continues to use is committing suicide. An overeater who continues to eat compulsively and destructively is committing suicide. Madness.

It is like a man standing in the town square stabbing himself with a knife and asking the passer--by, "Why am I bleeding?"

Today I accept my past destructive behavior and try to change it on a daily basis. Spirituality is loving yourself enough to see the writing on the wall and do something about it. Change is sanity for the madman!

God, You seem to have given me a dose of insanity.
Let me use it to Your glory.

> *"A society that gives to one class all the opportunities for leisure, and to another class all the burdens of work, dooms both classes to spiritual sterility."*

> *Lewis Mumford*

Spirituality brings with it balance. In order to be relaxed, healthy and alive, I need both work and leisure. For me I need to remember it is okay to take a day off; to stay in and relax is not a waste; play time is creative time!

I was not only compulsive around alcohol and people but I was also obsessive about work. I was — and am — a work--aholic. I need to remember to H.A.L.T.: Don't get too Hungry. Don't get too Angry. Don't get too Lonely. Don't get too Tired.

Work for me can be a form of escape. In leisure I have the opportunity to meet with myself.

Go on — enjoy yourself, with yourself!

You, who made me a laborer in the vineyard, also expected me to sit and enjoy it.

> *"It is not necessary to get away from human nature but to alter its inner attitude of heart and mind."*
>
> J. F. Newton

An understanding of sobriety and serenity that has proved helpful to me is that we are not only changing but involved in change. We determine the results of the change.

I can change for good or bad. I can stay sober or drink. I can be cheerful and creative or negative and destructive. My attitude determines the results of my changing life.

Spirituality has been given, but it also needs to be nurtured. I need to surround myself with loving and honest people if I am to allow my spirituality to grow in my life. My continued willingness is essential to my sobriety and serenity.

Thank You for making me with a mind and heart that together create the action.

LEO BOOTH

He's a different kind of priest who says you don't have to be religious to be spiritual. The dynamic Englishman is a spiritual 'rebel with a cause': He wants to bring spirituality back into religion, and help the essence of being real and human. An energetic mix of Charlie Chaplin with a touch of Dudley Moore, he's an Episcopal priest who's as likely to quote The Velveteen Rabbit as often as the Bible. He's not afraid to tweak the noses of religious and psychotherapy establishments to get his message across, but once he's heard, he treats his listeners with warmth, dignity, compassion and insight.

For nearly two decades, he has focused on helping people reclaim their spiritual power. A recovering alcoholic and certified addictions and eating disorders counselor, he is a national consultant to treatment programs and organizations. Rev. Booth is an active Episcopal priest in the Diocese of Los Angeles. He is the author of 6 books on the issues of spirituality and recovery.

371

BOOKS BY LEO BOOTH

THE ANGEL AND THE FROG

In this charming spiritual fable, Cedric the Frog and the residents of Olde Stable Farm meet an angel named Christine and discover the Spiritual Process.

SCP Limited

THE GOD GAME — IT'S YOUR MOVE:
Reclaim Your Spiritual Power

We don't "get" spiritual. Our spirituality is built into us at creation, in the connection between Mental, Physical and Emotional. Claiming our spiritual power involves connecting to ourselves and learning to make our spiritually powerful moves.

Stillpoint Publishing

WHEN GOD BECOMES A DRUG:
Breaking the Chains of
Religious Addiction and Abuse

This challenging and insightful look at the symptoms and sources of religious addiction and abuse is also a guide to attaining healthy spirituality.

Putnam\Perigee

OTHER MATERIALS FROM
LEO BOOTH

40 INDIVIDUAL AUDIOS
and AUDIO ALBUMS (4 titles per set)

Individual audios and album sets on spirituality, religious abuse, self-empowerment, drug and alcohol abuse, codependency, relationship and life issues.

VIDEOS

An excellent addition to your recovery library, especially for treatment programs, hospitals, alcohol and drug councils. Each approximately 55 minutes running time.

V1   Say Yes To Life

V2   Meditations For Compulsive
       People

V3   Spirituality and Adult Children
       of Alcoholics Recovery

V4   Creating Healthy Relationships

V5   Recovery From An
       Eating Disorder

V6   Intervention: Creating
       an Opportunity to Live

V7   Overcoming Religious Addiction
       and Religious Abuse

V8   An Evening With Father Leo

ANNUAL SPIRITUAL EMPOWERMENT CONFERENCE CRUISES AND RETREATS

Each year, Leo Booth presents conference cruises and retreats. During these fun-filled days, you'll explore all aspects of healthy spirituality, from the morning "Attitude of Gratitude" meeting to the evening dancing and play. Themes include manifesting your life's dreams, achieving goals, claiming spiritual power and healing spiritual wounds of addictions or other issues. Dates and itineraries vary from year to year. Space is limited and fills up quickly, so early reservations are recommended.

CONFERENCES * WORKSHOPS INSERVICES * CONSULTANCIES

Leo Booth works with a variety of groups and organizations, from treatment centers and therapists, to the general public, teaching how to create healthy spirituality. The Spiritual Concepts staff will help you with any phase of the event, from choosing a topic to suggesting marketing strategies and creating ads and copy. If you would like to share his wit, wisdom and zest for life with your program or organization call Spiritual Concepts.

FOR A COMPLETE CATALOG AND INFORMATION CALL:

Spiritual Concepts

(800) 284-2804
(8:00 AM - 4:00 PM Pacific time
Monday - Friday)

2700 St. Louis Avenue
Long Beach, CA 90806

Internet: www.fatherleo.com

E-Mail: frleo@deltanet.com

INDEX

379